❇ ❇ ❇ ❇ ❇ ❇ ❇ ❇ ❇ ❇ ❇ ❇ ❇ ❇ ❇

Good Old-Fashioned Maine Cookery

Terry Rohe
and
Sally Cohen

P **Prima Publishing**
P.O. Box 1260BK
Rocklin, CA 95677

© 1994 by Terry Rohe

Production by Tobi Giannone, Bookman Productions
Composition by Janet Hansen, Alphatype
Copyediting by Carol Ann Sheffield
Interior design by Suzanne Montazer, Bookman Productions
Cover design by The Dunlavey Studio, Sacramento
Cover illustration by Stephanie Langley

Library of Congress Cataloging-in-Publication Data

Rohe, Terry.
    Good old-fashioned Maine cookery / Terry Rohe &
Sally Cohen.
        p.   cm.
    "From red flannel hash to Maine lobster stew—here is
a collection of 195 traditional Down East recipes."
    Includes index.
    ISBN 1-55958-430-0
    1. Cookery, American—New England style.   2. Cook-
ery—Maine.   I. Cohen, Sally.   II. Title.
    TX715.2.N48R65   1994
    641.59741—dc20   93-33001
                                                                        CIP

94 95 96 97 98 99 RRD 10 9 8 7 6 5 4 3 2 1

Printed in the United States of America

How to Order:

Single copies may be ordered from Prima Publishing, P.O. Box 1260BK, Rocklin, CA 95677; telephone (916) 786-0426. Quantity discounts are also available. On your letterhead, include information concerning the intended use of the books and the number of books you wish to purchase.

Acknowledgments

To families and friends who, over the years, have contributed their cherished recipes to the baskets of dog-eared clippings, paper scraps, envelope backs, and grocery lists that made up our original source material for this book, we give our love and our thanks.

Terry's particular gratitude goes to a Chinese cook named Ivan, lord of her kitchen in Shanghai, who allowed her to sneak into his domain (verboten territory for a young girl) and started her on the road to doing what she loves to do above all else—cook!

Sally's thanks go to her four children and her six grandchildren for having such open minds, even when they were small, on the subject of food. She's had few picky eaters, and that's what has made cooking such fun. And special thanks to Mimi Duffy for fitting Sally in and being right on target. To her husband, Peter, who made lunches and dinners, did laundry, marketing, and proofreading so that the deadlines could be met, she gives her love and gratitude. Somehow, whatever Sally's goals, he always assumes she can achieve them.

Contents

Introduction

There are three basic types of people in Maine: Summer People, who own or rent houses during the summer months; People "From Away," who live here but were born somewhere else; and Mainers, those who were lucky enough to have been born within the state's boundaries.

There's a story that illustrates perfectly the often ambivalent relationships among those who spend at least part of their time in this unique and magnificent place. The story involves a woman whose family had been coming to Maine each summer long before she was born. She loved it so much she eventually moved here, married, and in time had a lovely little daughter. Several weeks after the baby's birth, she happened to have the infant with her when she went to pick something up at the hardware store. The fifth-generation Mainer behind the cash register smiled and said, "That's a real cunnin' baby you have thayah."

"Well," she replied, "I understand *I'll* never be a Native Mainer, but at least my daughter is one."

Without looking up, the storeowner counted out her change. "You know," he said, "just because your cat has kittens in the oven, that doesn't make 'em biscuits!"

We are two women "From Away" who share a love of Maine and a love of cooking. It was only a matter of time before we began to learn some of the native recipes as we experimented with the bounty this glorious state serves up from her fields and the sea. Occasionally our recipes incorporate some of what we brought with us from years of cooking in our pre-Maine lives, but most of these dishes are just what the title of our book implies: Good Old-Fashioned Maine Cookery.

Terry, born in Siberia and raised in Shanghai, lived most of her mature life in New Orleans, where she was a professional television journalist for many years. She did a daily 90-minute news and feature program for NBC, and a cooking segment was always part of every show. She and Chef Paul Prudhomme even opened a cooking school together.

Sally has simply loved cooking all her life, from the time she baked her first apple pie at the age of seven and tripped with it in her hands on the way to the dining room. Most of her pie ended up in the dog's dish, but the desire to cook never waned. Although she designed and manufactured needlework kits for many years and also worked as a journalist, cooking was her first love and explains why she opened a catering business when she and her husband moved to Maine.

Our backgrounds help explain the eclectic nature of *Good Old-Fashioned Maine Cookery*. We have taken the wonderful traditional foods and recipes we found here and brought to them our own life experience. Many of the recipes, however, are reproduced exactly as they have been for generations. Only a fool would mess around with Lobster Stew! And always we have tried to remain faithful to the wonderful traditions and spirit of Down East Maine. For even though we are "From Away," our cookbook was born here!

Terry Rohe and Sally Cohen
Hancock and East Sullivan, Maine
December 1993

Eggs and Breakfast

We think breakfast gets short shrift in today's
world. People are in such a rush! Grab an oatmeal cookie, fill up your magnetic, nonspill
coffee mug, and spend the next twenty minutes on the road. There has to be a better way.

Following are some of the most wonderful
methods of beginning the day that we could
think of. Granted, most of them take a bit
more time than many folks can spend on cooking first thing in the morning, but there are
always the weekends. And we start the chapter
with a couple of suggestions for those of you
who eat breakfast on the run. It must be the
mother in us, but we can't bear to send you off
on an empty stomach!

1

Yogurt and Fruit

1 cup of your favorite flavor yogurt
½ cup fresh raspberries, strawberries, cut-up apple, or pear
    . . . you name it

Combine in a covered 2-cup plastic cup.

❋ ❋ ❋

*It was the end of August. A summer visitor walked into
Alley's store and while getting some groceries said, "You
got a lot of odd people around here."*

"Won't have after Labor Day."

Yogurt and Cereal

1 cup apple-cinnamon yogurt
1 cup apple-cinnamon Cheerios

Combine in a covered 2-cup plastic cup.

Variation:

1 cup banana yogurt
½ banana, sliced
¼ cup Grape Nuts or Granola

Combine in a covered 2-cup plastic cup.

Banana Bread and Cream Cheese

The night before, prepare a sandwich of 2 slices banana bran bread spread with cream cheese.

Now come our recipes for lazy weekends and company brunches.

❇ ❇ ❇

A man from away pulled up to the curb and said,
"Can I take this road to Portland?"

"Guess you can. But I figure they got plenty
of them up there already."

Parsley Oysters à la Alice

Parsley needs a cold, damp environment, and Maine often complies. It's a great crop for your salad garden and loves to grow indoors on your kitchen window sill in the winter. The following recipe is a delectable way to make one egg go a long way.

Alice Doerr, whose recipe this is, tells me she puts ginger in most things that cause gas, such as broccoli, parsley, or cauliflower. Alice lived for many years in Digby, Nova Scotia, where she designed and built a solar heating system for her house and raised asparagus for the local hotel and markets, two projects most people said were going to prove impossible to accomplish. The word "impossible" was always like a starter's gun to Alice. Her solar heating system was featured in two Canadian national magazines, and we can personally attest to the succulence of her asparagus. When she and Herb Doerr married, they "moved South" to Maine. The following is a recipe for one person.

1 egg, lightly beaten
½ cup parsley, chopped, without stems
salt and pepper to taste
pinch ground ginger
1 tablespoon butter

Mix the egg and the parsley. Add the salt, pepper, and ginger. Melt the butter in the bottom of a skillet. Drop the egg mixture by the tablespoonful into the skillet. When browned on one side, turn over and brown the other side. Each egg will make about 5 "oysters."

Serves 1.

Eggs Benedict à l'Orange

This is one of the most luscious brunch dishes imaginable. Once or twice a year, forget about fats and cholesterol and treat yourselves and some guests to a real culinary gem. The orange hollandaise sauce is what makes this even more special.

4 slices Canadian bacon
2 whole wheat English muffins (4 halves)
1/4 cup frozen orange juice concentrate
1/4 cup water
1 stick butter
4 extra-large eggs
3 egg yolks
4 orange slices

In a nonstick skillet, lightly brown the Canadian bacon. Drain and keep warm. Toast the 4 English muffin halves and keep warm. Fill another nonstick skillet with water and bring it to a simmer.

While the water is heating, mix the orange juice concentrate and 1/4 cup water and heat with the butter until the butter is melted. Break the 4 eggs, one by one, into a cup and slide each egg into the simmering water. Continue to simmer them until they are just firm, about 2 to 3 minutes.

While the eggs are poaching, place the egg yolks in the container of a blender and blend for a few seconds. With the motor running, pour in the hot orange butter in a slow, steady stream. The sauce will thicken as you pour.

Quickly remove the eggs from the hot water and place them on a warm plate. Place one half-slice of English muffin on each of four plates. Place a slice of Canadian bacon on top of each muffin slice and then place one of the poached eggs on top of the bacon. Pour some of the hollandaise sauce over each egg, garnish with an orange slice, and serve.

Serves 4.

❆ ❆ ❆

Asked a fellow in Jonesport if he'd lived there all his life.

"Not yet," he said.

Hearty Scrambled Eggs

2 tablespoons butter
1 medium red onion, halved, then thinly sliced
1 small green pepper
1 tablespoon shallots, chopped
3 green onions (scallions) finely diced, whites and first ⅓ of
    the greens
1 clove garlic, finely minced
1 cup red potatoes, cooked and diced, skins on
1 medium tomato, skin on, seeded and diced
salt and black pepper to taste
pinch cayenne pepper
½ cup thinly sliced ham, shredded (optional)
4 eggs, lightly beaten with 2 tablespoons water

Heat a 10- or 12-inch nonstick skillet. Add the butter and
sauté the red onion, green pepper, shallots, green onions,
and garlic for 1 or 2 minutes or until soft, stirring often.
Add the potato cubes and sauté another minute. Add the
tomato, salt, pepper, cayenne, and ham (if desired). Add
the eggs and cook, moving the eggs away from the edges
and toward the center of the pan. Cook until just set. Serve
on a hot platter surrounded by Corn Sticks (recipe
follows).

Serves 4 hearty eaters.

Corn Sticks

1 cup white cornmeal
$\frac{1}{2}$ cup cracker meal
1 teaspoon baking powder
$\frac{1}{2}$ teaspoon salt
1 teaspoon sugar
1 egg, lightly beaten
$\frac{3}{4}$ cup milk
$\frac{1}{4}$ cup melted butter

Sift the dry ingredients together. Mix the egg and the milk. Combine egg mixture with the dry ingredients gradually, keeping the mixture stiff. Stir in the butter and mix thoroughly. Mold into finger-length sticks, about 1 inch in diameter, on a cutting board dusted with cracker meal. Bake on a greased cookie sheet in a preheated 450° oven until brown, about 10 to 15 minutes.

Makes 12 to 15 sticks.

❈ ❈ ❈

A summer visitor walked into the local general store and asked the owner how business was. He says, "Well, Monday I sold a case of sardines. Didn't do nuthin' Tuesday. Wednesday the fella brought back the case of sardines. So I guess you could say Tuesday was my best day."

Cinnamon French Toast

The trick here is the unsliced bread. You can make the portions as voluptuously thick and decadant as you want.

1 loaf unsliced cinnamon swirl bread
4 eggs
1/4 cup milk
1 teaspoon vanilla
dash nutmeg
dash cinnamon
2 to 3 tablespoons butter
100% pure maple syrup (topping)

Cut 8 slices of the bread, each about 1 inch thick. Break the eggs into a wide, shallow bowl or a pie plate. Add the milk, vanilla, nutmeg, and cinnamon. Heat a large nonstick frying pan and melt 1 tablespoon of the butter in it. Dip the bread slices in the egg mixture and fry them in the butter over medium heat until nicely browned. Flip them over, brown the other sides, remove from the pan, and keep warm on a plate in a 200° oven while you cook the rest of the slices. Serve with crisp bacon and maple syrup.

Serves 4.

Finnish Pancakes

This, as its name implies, is an import, but one that has achieved real (if modest) celebrity Down East. The blueberries are a recent addition.

1 cup milk
⅓ cup whole wheat flour
⅓ cup white flour
½ teaspoon salt
2 eggs
½ teaspoon grated lemon zest
½ teaspoon ground cardamom
2 ounces (½ stick) butter or margarine
¾ cup Maine wild blueberries

Place all the ingredients except the butter and blueberries in a blender. Blend, then scrape down the sides of the container. Place the butter in a 9-inch pie plate and melt in a preheated 400° oven. Add the berries to the batter, but do not blend. Mix in gently with a wooden spoon. Pour the batter into the pie plate. Bake in the 400° oven until it puffs up and turns golden brown. Serve hot with blueberry sauce or syrup.

Serves 4.

Cheese Soufflé

Once you've actually made a soufflé and understand the process, you'll really enjoy putting them together and trying out lots of different dessert soufflés as well as savory ones such as the cheese soufflé below. We chose this one because it is simple, because cheese is used so often in Maine cookery, and because it's so good.

*A soufflé is basically a cream sauce, flavoring (in this case Cheddar cheese), and stiffly beaten egg whites. You can do everything up to the egg white part ahead of time. You **must** decide exactly when you want to serve the meal, because tides and soufflés wait for no one. The good news is that even a dropped soufflé tastes wonderful.*

3 tablespoons butter
3 tablespoons flour
1 cup milk
¼ teaspoon cayenne pepper
¼ teaspoon salt
dash Worcestershire sauce
½ pound Cheddar cheese, grated
3 eggs, separated

In a 2-quart saucepan, melt the butter, add the flour, and stir with a wire whisk until blended. Bring the milk to a boil in another saucepan and add it to the flour mixture all at once, stirring briskly to make sure there are no lumps. When smooth, add cayenne, salt, and Worcestershire and mix well. Remove the sauce from the heat and let it cool for a few minutes. Add the cheese and stir until it is melted. Beat in the egg yolks one at a time.

The soufflé may be prepared up to this point and held for several hours in the refrigerator. If you do this, bring back to room temperature before proceeding.

Beat the egg whites until they hold peaks, but stop before they become dry. Fold the whites into the cheese mixture and turn into a 2-quart soufflé dish. Place the dish in a preheated 400° oven for 20 minutes. Then reduce the heat to 350° and bake until the top is nicely browned, about 10 to 15 minutes more. Serve immediately.

Serves 4 or 5.

※ ※ ※

When the foreman of the sardine factory in Yarmouth was asked how many men worked there, he sez, " 'Bout half."

Bagels and Lox

OKAY, OKAY! So this is not a Down East recipe. But you can buy wonderful fresh bagels in a nearly infinite number of varieties (including Maine wild blueberry at the local Shop and Save), and the smoked salmon (lox to many people) **is** *a native treat. Squeeze yourself a glass of fresh orange juice, brew some freshly ground coffee, and enjoy one of the world's great breakfasts.*

1 bagel, split and toasted
cream cheese
fresh smoked salmon, thinly sliced
a few capers or chopped fresh dill (optional)

Spread the toasted bagel with the cream cheese. Top with a slice of the smoked salmon and garnish with a few capers or chopped fresh dill, if desired.

Serves 1.

❋ ❋ ❋

A fellow in the middle of what appeared to be a small town asked the way to Dover Foxcroft. The answer was, "Don't you move a damned inch!"

Pecan Waffles

It's nice to know that there are some delicious recipes that can be made lowfat, low cholesterol without losing anything in the translation. Waffles, pancakes, and crepes are such dishes, and if you or someone you know is really trying to watch such things, here is one of the wonderful recipes you can enjoy.

2 cups buttermilk
½ cup egg substitute (Egg Beaters is one brand)
2 tablespoons sugar or honey
2 tablespoons canola oil
½ cup whole wheat flour
1½ cups white flour
pinch salt
1 teaspoon baking soda
½ cup chopped pecan pieces

Preheat your waffle iron and spray all cooking surfaces with vegetable spray. In a medium bowl, mix the buttermilk, egg substitute, honey (if used), and oil. In a large bowl, mix the whole wheat and white flours, salt, baking soda, and sugar (if used). Add the buttermilk mixture to the flour mixture and stir until blended. Add the nuts, stir briefly, and cook for about 2 minutes per waffle (or follow waffle iron directions).

Serves 4.

Quiche Lorraine

A quiche is basically a pie or a tart filled with an egg custard that contains one or two other main ingredients. There are savory quiches and there are sweet (dessert) quiches. A dessert quiche usually has a couple of tablespoons of sugar in the crust. Quiche making can be an art form. They are lots of fun to bake from scratch, but we're taking some shortcuts here so we can penetrate the mystique and show you how easy and satisfying a savory quiche can be.

4 slices lean bacon, fried, drained, and crumbled into bits
1 small onion, finely diced
bacon fat left on skillet after remainder has been poured off
1 9-inch preformed pastry shell
1 cup Swiss cheese, diced in small cubes
2 tablespoons grated Romano cheese
3 eggs, beaten
2 cups light or heavy cream
¼ teaspoon nutmeg, freshly ground if possible
salt and white pepper to taste

Preheat the oven to 375°. After you have removed the cooked bacon from the skillet, put the onion into whatever fat remains after you have drained the skillet. Sauté until the onions are soft and golden. Place the pie crust in a 9-inch pie or tart pan. Sprinkle the bacon, onion, and cheeses over the crust. Combine the eggs, cream, nutmeg, salt, and pepper and pour them over the cheese mixture. Bake at 375° until a knife inserted 1½ inches from the side of the pastry comes out clean, about 25 to 30 minutes.

Serves 6.

Starters and Snacks

Mainers are hearty eaters. They have to be, with so much work to do. When we moved Down East, our friends "from away" used to ask, "But what do you *do* all winter, after all the summer people have gone? Doesn't it get boring? Isn't it lonely?" Our answer has always been, "There aren't enough hours in the day to do everything that needs to be done to get through the winter and ready for the spring."

During the long winter we also are able to get together with the good friends whom we have not had an opportunity to see all summer. Often we invite each other to share a dinner. Dinnertime in Maine can be as early as 5:30 P.M. and is almost never later than 6:30. After all, it's dark by 4:00. Sometimes we get together to rent a VCR movie. The nearest theater is a 30-mile round trip.

Dinner usually comprises a starter, a main course, and a dessert. Movies are generally accompanied by a snack. Hors d'oeuvres are usually reserved for large parties.

Following is a cross-section of robust starters and snacks that have received good reviews from friends with hearty appetites.

Broiled Stuffed Mushrooms

We buy the big, fat supermarket mushrooms for stuffing, but every August and September we hunt and harvest wild chanterelles from the woods in Hancock and chop them up to add to the stuffing mix. No, we won't tell you the best spots to find them; besides, one almost never finds them in the same place twice. And unless you're an expert, be sure to check with someone who is before eating wild mushrooms you've harvested.

12 large mushrooms
3 tablespoons butter
1 small onion, finely diced
1 clove garlic, pressed
$\frac{1}{3}$ cup fresh tomatoes, finely chopped
$\frac{3}{4}$ cup seasoned bread crumbs
2 tablespoons sherry
1 tablespoon grated Parmesan cheese
$\frac{1}{2}$ cup fresh crabmeat

Preheat broiler. Wipe the mushrooms with a damp paper towel and dice the stems finely. Melt 2 tablespoons of the butter in a medium skillet and sauté chopped stems, onion, and garlic until soft, about 2 minutes. Add the rest of the ingredients, mix, and sauté until well blended.

Place the mushroom caps, brushed with the remaining butter, cavities down on a baking sheet and broil about 2 minutes, watching carefully to see that they don't burn. Invert the caps, fill with the stuffing, and broil about 3 minutes longer.

Serves 4 to 6.

Angels on Horseback or Bacon-Wrapped Oysters

Simple to put together, and the flavors are so wonderfully complementary. Make sure your toothpick catches both the bacon and the oyster. If you shuck your own oysters, please be very careful; it takes a while to get the hang of it. Ask the person at your fish market for a quick demonstration. The tiny, saber-shaped shucking knives are available in specialty shops.

pepper
12 large oysters, shucked
6 slices lean bacon
toast squares

Preheat oven to 450°. Pepper the oysters and wrap each one in a half slice of bacon. Secure each with a toothpick. Bake in a 450° oven until the bacon crisps, or broil carefully enough to avoid scorching the bacon. Serve on the toast squares.

Serves 4 to 6.

Marion's Cheese Wafers

Marion Wise has been cooking up a storm for over fifty years. She has coaxed a magnificent English garden out of the rocky Maine coast; her lush herb garden grows and multiplies deep into every chilly autumn. This recipe was the first of many she has shared with us over the years. They will store for weeks in a tightly covered tin or well wrapped in the freezer. Small children take note: they look like cookies, but the cayenne gives them a real kick!

3 cups all-purpose flour, sifted
2 teaspoons baking powder
½ teaspoon salt
1 heaping teaspoon cayenne pepper
½ pound (2 sticks) butter
4 cups (1 pound) sharp Cheddar cheese, grated
whole pecans (optional)

Sift the dry ingredients. Cream the butter and grated cheese and mix with the dry ingredients to make a dough. Refrigerate at least 1 hour. Roll the dough ¼ inch thick on a floured board. Cut with a floured cookie cutter into any shape that suits your fancy. Place a pecan on top if desired. Preheat oven to 375° and bake for 10 to 13 minutes, depending on your oven and the size of the biscuits. They are golden brown when done.

Serves 15 to 20.

Denise's Delicious Dip

Denise Malm and her architect husband, Rick, have a couple of active youngsters and love this recipe because you can make it when you have a spare half hour and serve it as long as a day later. It's so hearty, it's all you need for a party hors d'oeuvre.
   We thought it sounded a little weird when we first read the recipe, but wait till you taste it! This dip is good for large groups because you can easily make 50 percent more or even double it. Serve on veggies, pita bread, crackers, or whatever.

1 pound cream cheese, softened
2 tablespoons lemon juice
dash garlic powder
1 tablespoon snipped fresh chives
1/4 cup mayonnaise
1 teaspoon Worcestershire sauce
1/2 cup celery, finely chopped
2 tablespoons green or red relish
3/4 cup chili sauce
1/2 pound fresh crabmeat
1/4 pound cooked Maine shrimp

Beat together the above ingredients, except for the relish, chili sauce, crab, and shrimp. Spread to form a 9-inch circle on a platter. Chill.
   Combine the relish and chili sauce. Spread over the cream cheese round. Return to the refrigerator.
   Mix together the crabmeat and shrimp. If you can find only larger shrimp, dice them. Arrange over the top layer, cover with plastic wrap, and chill until ready to serve with your crackers, veggies, or whatever you please.

Serves 15 to 20.

Connie's Spicy Nuts

Even though these are sweet, they are a nice appetizer. Just as good to munch on while watching Casablanca.

½ cup sugar
½ teaspoon vanilla
¼ cup water
½ teaspoon ground cinnamon
pinch salt
8 ounces walnuts or pecans

Put the ingredients, except for the nuts, in a nonstick skillet and bring to a rolling boil. Boil about 5 minutes or until a firm ball forms when a few drops are poured into cold water. Watch carefully or the sugar will burn. Remove from the heat and stir in the nuts. When cool, the nuts will be coated with the spicy sugar.

Serves 10 or more, depending on how many other choices of appetizer you have.

✳ ✳ ✳

"Think it's going to stop raining?"

"Always has."

Smoked Fish Mousse

Smoked fish is plentiful in Maine. There are scores of local fishermen who smoke it and sell it to the many little general stores as well as to the supermarkets. It almost doesn't matter what kind of fish you use—it's fun to try different ones. Our personal favorites are trout or haddock.

1 pound smoked fish fillet, bones removed
1 tablespoon shallots, minced
1 tablespoon chopped dill
½ teaspoon white pepper
⅛ teaspoon grated nutmeg
1 tablespoon gelatin
2 cups heavy cream
1 tablespoon brandy

Skin the fish and make sure all the bones have been removed. Puree in a food processor with the shallots and seasonings. Dissolve the gelatin in the cream. Add the brandy and heat until you no longer feel grittiness under your spoon. Pour into the processor over the fish and process 6 or 7 seconds longer.

Pour into a lightly oiled 3-cup fish mold or other mold. Chill 6 to 8 hours or overnight. Sponge the bottom of the mold with warm water and unmold upon a bed of lettuce or decorate with fresh dill.

Serves 15 to 20.

Shrimp and Curried Cream Cheese on Cucumber Rounds

These looks so elegant and professional that everyone will think a caterer did them for you. Yet they are easy and quick (and fun to do). We bet you'll make them often. Kids love to use a pastry bag, so show them how and let them pipe the shrimp mixture onto the cucumber.

½ pound Maine or other shrimp
1 tablespoon water
8 ounces cream cheese
milk as needed
2 tablespoons white wine
curry powder to taste
2 firm cucumbers, sliced into rounds

Clean and peel the shrimp. Maine shrimp do not have to be deveined, but the larger varieties should be. Place the shrimp and water in a microwavable dish and cover with plastic wrap. Cook for 1 minute on high power (longer for a lower-powered microwave) or until the shrimp turn pink. If using large shrimp, cut them into 1-inch chunks.

Mix the cream cheese with a little milk and the wine until it is softened. Mix with the curry powder. Put the cream cheese mixture in a pastry bag with a large star tip and pipe onto each cucumber round. Place 1 shrimp on top of each round.

Serves 15 or more.

Spicy Meatballs with Spicy Tomato Sauce

1 pound lean ground beef
½ cup Italian seasoned bread crumbs
¼ cup spaghetti sauce
1 teaspoon chili powder
1 small onion, finely minced
1 egg, lightly beaten

Mix all the ingredients together in a large bowl. Form into balls about 1¼ to 1½ inches in diameter. They will shrink slightly when baked. Put the balls on a cookie sheet and bake at 350° for 20 minutes or until done.

Pour Spicy Tomato Sauce over the meatballs and serve hot, with toothpicks.

Serves 6 to 8.

Spicy Tomato Sauce

2 cups tomato sauce
¼ cup dark brown sugar
juice of 1 lemon
4 or 5 drops Tabasco sauce
½ teaspoon garlic powder
salt and pepper to taste
1 teaspoon chili powder
1 teaspoon onion flakes

Mix all the ingredients together in a small saucepan. Cook over low heat for 10 minutes. Pour over the meatballs in a casserole and heat in the oven at 350° until hot.

Serves 6 to 8.

Baked Spiced Smelt

This recipe was an intriguing surprise to us. It is aromatic and wonderful and a perfect first course or hors d'oeuvre.

2 pounds smelts, ready to cook
2 large onions, thinly sliced
2 cloves garlic, chopped
2 carrots, grated
2 bay leaves
2 peppercorns
5 lemon slices
½ cup olive oil
½ cup wine vinegar
salt to taste
1 teaspoon paprika
1 teaspoon each allspice, cloves, and cinnamon, mixed
2 cups water
1 cup white wine

Arrange the fish on a large baking dish. Combine all the other ingredients in a pan and bring to a boil. Simmer for 15 minutes. Pour this sauce over the fish and bake at 400° for 12 to 15 minutes. Cool and serve chilled.

Serves 8 to 10 as an hors d'oeuvre.

Smoked Atlantic Salmon

½ loaf black bread or 1 loaf dark party rye bread
¼ pound Saga cheese with herbs
¼ pound smoked salmon, thinly sliced
4 or 5 sprigs fresh dill weed, washed and dried

If using black bread, cut the slices into quarters. If using party rye, use the slices as they come. Spread each piece of bread with a thin layer of cheese. Place a bit of salmon on top and add a small sprig of dill over the salmon. Cover with plastic wrap and refrigerate until ready to serve.

Makes 12 to 15 appetizers.

❊ ❊ ❊

While picking up his mail, a visitor from New Jersey said to the postmaster, "You sure got a lot of old folk up here. What's your mortality rate?"

"Just like it's always been . . . one per person."

Stuffed Deviled Eggs

*The rule of thumb is three appetizers per person if you are
having three or four selections. We always find that the deviled
eggs disappear first. Forewarned is forearmed!*

6 large eggs, hard-boiled and halved
3 or 4 tablespoons mayonnaise
1 teaspoon dry mustard
1/4 teaspoon Worcestershire sauce
dash cayenne pepper
4 or 5 green olives, stuffed with pimento, chopped

Gently scrape the yolks out of the eggs and into a small
bowl. Add the first 3 tablespoons of mayonnaise, the mustard, Worcestershire sauce, pepper, and olives. Mix thoroughly. If it seems too stiff, add the last tablespoon of
mayonnaise. Place the yolk mixture back into the whites'
cavities, either by spooning it in or by placing the mixture
in a pastry bag with a large star tip and piping it in.

Serves 4.

Crabmeat Puffs

1 tablespoon onion, grated
¼ cup cream cheese, softened
¼ cup mayonnaise
1 tablespoon chives, chopped
3 drops Tabasco sauce
¼ pound crabmeat
4 slices white bread, crusts removed, quartered and lightly toasted

Mix together the onion, cream cheese, mayonnaise, chives, and Tabasco. Fold in the crabmeat. Spread on the toast squares and place under a preheated broiler for 2 to 3 minutes or until puffed up and golden brown.

Serves 4 to 6.

Josh and Oscar were sitting in front of the general store whittling.

Oscar says, "What's new?"

"Nawthin' much!" Josh answers. "Got a new hoss for my wife."

"Damn good trade."

Cheddar Cheese and Chutney

Somehow this always reminds us of Christmas. It's a lovely appetizer to serve before a roaring fire with a glass of port or sherry.

crackers
4 ounces Cheddar with port wine cheese
¼ cup your favorite chutney

Spread the crackers with the cheese. Top with a little mound of chutney.

Serves 4 to 6.

❊ ❊ ❊

"You got a criminal lawyer over your way?"

"We think so, but we haven't been able to prove nawthin' on him yet."

Soups and Chowders

Soups occupy a special place in our hearts and in this book because Maine has a long, cold winter season. We're on the seacoast and have dozens of inland lakes and streams, so fish soups and chowders hold a preeminent place in our cuisine.

We could think of no better way to start this chapter than to reprint the Turtle Island Fish Chowder recipe from *Summer Secrets,* a slim cookbook published by The Church of the Redeemer in neighboring Sorrento, Maine. The recipe and its introduction were written by our friend Ellen Devine, whose family members have been summer residents for over a century, a fact that helps explain why so many of her relatives were actually born here.

Turtle Island Fish Chowder

The Ewing–Noyes–Stone–Devine chowder picnics began in vast confusion on the town dock with three or four boats, an army's equipment, a crew of thirty or forty people, and a few privileged dogs. Usually the very young, the very old, the seasick, and a master chowder maker (with assistants) were deposited on Turtle Island. They started the fire, peeled and chopped, wandered in the woods and the meadow, and explored tidal pools.

The fishermen left for Egg Rock under the command of Old Bill Andrews or Willie Bunker, with Stewart Andrews, fisherman and clam shucker sans pareil. There they rocked on the sunny swells, gripping their thick lines with salty, soggy gloves, encouraged by the promise of a quarter for the first, a quarter for the most and a quarter for the biggest. If they were skunked, the fastest craft was dispatched to Bar Harbor for "fish caught on a silver hook." With luck, the flotilla returned triumphant, in a cloud of gulls as they cleaned their catch.

After a feast of chowder, wine, fruit, pies, and cakes on the sunny rocks, heading home was tough. Few were awake to hear the welcoming Sorrento bell buoy.

2 pounds salt pork (or more)
1 5-pound bag (or more) onions
1 5-pound bag (or more) bite-size potatoes (if bigger, cut to fit)
6 pounds fillet of haddock, cusk, cod, or other firm white fish
1 gallon whole milk
salt and pepper to taste
1 pint heavy cream

¾ stick butter
Pilot crackers
small sweet pickles

Cut the salt pork into crouton-size pieces (they shrink).
Brown them, stirring frequently, in a heavy skillet or
electric frying pan. Remove with a spatula to paper towels
to drain. Cook the onions in the salt pork fat until
transparent.

Meanwhile, simmer the potatoes in a little water or
clam broth until almost done. Add the drained onions and
fish fillets on top. Simmer until the fish is almost done
and starts to fall apart. Add the milk and quite a lot of salt
and pepper to taste. *Do not boil.* At the last minute, add the
cream to taste and float butter pats on top. Serve with the
pork croutons, Pilot crackers (oyster crackers), and sweet
pickles. It is better the next day and fine on the third day.

Serves 20 to 25.

✺ ✺ ✺

Tourist: "How far is it to Kennebunkport?"

Farmer: " 'Bout 26,000 miles, the way you're going."

Curried Corn and Tomato Soup

We use fresh corn when we can, but since corn season lasts about an hour and a half in Maine (and that's during a good summer), we cherish those golden corn-on-the-cob meals but generally revert to frozen for this soup. It's almost as good.

3 tablespoons butter, margarine, or canola oil
3 tablespoons flour
1 cup milk
1 teaspoon curry powder
$1/4$ teaspoon cayenne pepper
2 cups chicken stock
1 cup canned crushed tomatoes
1 teaspoon dried dill or 1 tablespoon fresh dill, minced
1 cup fresh or frozen corn kernels

Melt the butter or margarine, or pour oil into a large kettle or pot. Add the flour and stir with a whisk for 1 minute. Add the milk and whisk over medium heat until it thickens. Add the curry powder and cayenne; stir well. Add the chicken stock and crushed tomatoes. Add the dill and corn. Heat *just* to a simmer for 10 minutes, stirring occasionally. This soup is best when allowed to stand for a couple of hours to blend flavors. Heat well before serving.

Serves 4.

Lentil Soup

This is the one you want to have ready at the end of a day of cross-country skiing. It takes about 15 minutes to put it together followed by about 1 hour of slow cooking. It freezes beautifully, so make a double batch.

1 tablespoon oil
1 cup onion, diced
2 stalks celery, diced
1 carrot, diced
1 large clove garlic, minced
1 pound lentils, sorted and washed
1 cup tomatoes, crushed, canned or fresh
6 cups water or canned or homemade chicken stock
2 tablespoons butter or margarine
3 tablespoons flour
¼ cup red wine vinegar
½ pound precooked kielbasa sausage (we use Healthy
    Choice, making this a lowfat meal), cut in thin rounds

Heat the oil in a soup kettle or 5-quart saucepan. Add the onion, celery, carrot, and garlic and sauté until the vegetables are soft. Add the lentils, tomatoes, and water or stock, and simmer for about 1 hour or until the lentils are tender.

Melt the butter or margarine over medium heat and stir until it is a medium brown color. Add the flour and stir with a wire whisk for about 1 minute after turning the heat to low. Remove from the heat, add the vinegar, and stir into the soup. Stir over low heat until the soup has thickened. Add the sausage and heat till the sausage is warmed.

Serves 4 to 6.

Corn Chowder

This hearty chowder is perfect as is, but if you're in the mood for gilding the lily, just add a cup of fresh, picked crabmeat or scallops, and voilà, *a party meal when you add a salad and homemade bread.*

4 slices bacon
3 medium onions, sliced
4 medium potatoes, sliced, skins on
1½ cups fresh or frozen corn
1 beef bouillon cube
1 cup water
crabmeat or scallops (optional)
3 cups milk
salt and freshly ground pepper to taste

Fry the bacon until crisp. Drain and reserve it. Sauté the onions in bacon fat until tender, then transfer to a 3-quart saucepan along with the potatoes, corn, bouillon cube, and water. Cover and cook 15 minutes. Add crabmeat or scallops, if desired, and cook 2 minutes more. Add the milk and heat almost to the boiling point. Add salt and pepper, ladle into bowls, and garnish with the bacon, crumbled into pieces.

Serves 4 to 6.

Clam Chowder

Mother's milk to the folks Down East. Don't even mention the word tomato to a Mainer in the same breath as clam chowder. The Local product is made with milk. The red kind comes from The Big Apple.

⅛ pound salt pork (or 2 tablespoons butter or oil, but it
   won't taste the same)
1 medium onion, diced
1 cup potatoes, diced
salt and pepper to taste
1 pint minced sea clams (quahogs are the local product)
1 quart whole milk, scalded
pinch dried basil and/or oregano (optional)

Dice the salt pork and cook until crisp. Remove the pork and set aside. Sauté the onion in the pork fat, butter, or oil until golden. Add the potatoes and just enough water to cover. Season with the salt and pepper, cover, and bring to a boil. Turn down the heat and simmer until the potatoes are just tender. Add the clams, bring to a simmer again, and cook for just *2* minutes longer (pay attention . . . the price for making a phone call at this point is rubbery clams). Add the hot milk. Season to taste and serve piping hot, adding bits of pork scraps or dots of butter.

Serves 4.

French Clam Bisque

*Down East Maine is just a stone's throw from French-speaking
Canada, and the influence of French cooking is often evident.
This is a superb clam soup that found its way over the border.*

30 large cherrystone clams (or 1 pint shucked)
3 large onions
3 large garlic cloves
2 ounces (½ stick) butter
1 teaspoon saffron, crushed
¾ tablespoon fresh thyme, or 1 teaspoon dried
6 medium tomatoes
2½ cups dry white wine
1 cup rice
2 cups milk
1 cup heavy cream
Tabasco sauce
salt and pepper to taste

Scrub the clams, open, and reserve the liquid. Chop the
clams and add them to the liquid. Peel and chop the onions
and garlic. Heat the butter in a large pan. Add the onions,
garlic, saffron, and thyme. Sauté until the onions are transparent. Chop the tomatoes coarsely and add to the soup,
together with the wine and rice. Cover and simmer for
1 hour, stirring occasionally.

   Strain the liquid into a large saucepan. Place the clam-
tomato-rice mixture into a blender or food processor and
puree until smooth. Stir in the milk and cream; add the
Tabasco, salt, and pepper. Serve hot or cold with chopped
fresh thyme (if you have it) as a garnish.

Serves 6.

Turkey Bone Soup

In our neck of the woods, "waste not, want not" are truly words we live by. This delectable soup is an awesome example of that credo. What you put into it is not carved in granite . . . if you have some leftover veggies, toss 'em in. Be creative!

1 cooked turkey carcass
1 medium onion, sliced
water
1 tablespoon parsley, chopped
1 whole bay leaf
1 teaspoon dried sage (optional)
1 teaspoon dried thyme (optional)
dash ground cloves
1 cup turkey dressing (use a mix if you have none left over)
up to 2 cups turkey gravy
salt and pepper to taste

Scrape the meat from the turkey bones and set aside with the dressing. Break the bones into smallish pieces and place in a large soup kettle or stock pot. Add the onion slices and cover with cold water. Add herbs only if none were used in the dressing. Simmer on low heat for 3 hours.

Remove the bones, scrape them again, and cool the broth. When cold, skim the fat. Remove the bay leaf and add the dressing, meat, gravy, salt, and pepper. Add ½ cup more water for each pint of soup. Simmer at least 30 minutes more and serve.

Serves 6.

Maine Bouillabaisse

At first glance, it seems like an awful lot of bother, and there are a lot of ingredients in this incomparable dish. However, look at it this way: most of the makings are things you already have in your kitchen, and the esoteric ones like ouzo and saffron will be handy the next time you want one of the world's great taste treats.

1 8- or 10-ounce bottle clam juice
1 cup dry white wine
1 large onion, quartered
1 carrot, sliced
1 lemon slice (yes, just a single slice)
1 orange slice
1 small bay leaf
1/4 teaspoon thyme
1/4 teaspoon marjoram
1/4 teaspoon saffron threads, crushed
4 cups water
2 tablespoons virgin olive oil
3 large cloves garlic, minced
1 pound fresh tomatoes, coarsely chopped, or 1 cup
      canned crushed tomatoes
1 1/2 pounds firm white fish
1/4 pound medium shrimp, deveined and shelled (Maine
      shrimp need not be deveined)
1 dozen clams or mussels or both, scrubbed
1/3 cup parsley, chopped
2 tablespoons anisette or ouzo liqueur
1 teaspoon grated lemon zest
1/2 teaspoon salt (optional)

Assemble, measure, chop, and grate all the ingredients. In a large stainless steel or enameled pot, combine the clam juice, wine, onion, carrot, lemon slice, orange slice, bay leaf, thyme, marjoram, and saffron. Add the water and bring to a boil. Reduce the heat and simmer, uncovered, for 20 minutes.

Heat the oil in a large nonstick skillet and sauté the garlic and tomatoes until soft. Add them to the stock and simmer 6 or 7 minutes. Add the fish, shrimps, and clams and simmer for 6 minutes more, until the fish becomes opaque and the clams open. Add the parsley, anisette, lemon zest, and salt.

Serves 6 in large bowls.

❋ ❋ ❋

Fred Fowler's guernsey cow was hit by a pickup truck and killed. For the first time in his life, Fred was obliged to fill out an insurance form. Under the item "Disposition of Carcass" he wrote, "Kind and gentle."

Cream of Broccoli Soup

Broccoli is one of the major crops in Maine and is once again legal under the new Clinton administration. This soup is just as good served cold on a summer evening as it is poured into a thermos bottle and served as the starter on a sailing picnic.

1 medium onion, finely chopped
1 tablespoon butter
1 tablespoon vegetable oil
4 cups chicken broth, homemade or canned, fat removed
1 large russet potato, peeled and diced
2 cups broccoli
½ cup half-and-half
salt and white pepper to taste
¼ teaspoon grated nutmeg (fresh if possible)

In a 5- or 6-quart pot, sauté the onion in the butter and oil until soft. Add the broth and potatoes and simmer until the potatoes are soft. Add the broccoli and simmer another 4 or 5 minutes or until just tender. Put the soup, in 2-cup batches, into a blender and blend until smooth, returning the blended soup to a bowl. You may either blend the entire amount or reserve a cup with potato cubes and broccoli florets to add back at the end. When the soup is blended, return it to the cooking pot; add the half-and-half, salt, pepper, and nutmeg; and reheat but do not boil.

Serves 4.

Lamb Soup

Raising sheep was once a fairly large industry in Maine and is still done in some areas. Often the flocks were raised on an island, rendering fences unnecessary. Spring leg of lamb is one of life's great treats, and this soup allows you to get another meal out of a rather expensive dinner.

1 leftover meaty lamb leg
2 cups Chinese cabbage, chopped
2 tomatoes, cubed
$\frac{1}{2}$ cup peas
$\frac{1}{2}$ cup corn
3 potatoes, skins on, scrubbed and cubed
$\frac{3}{4}$ cup mushrooms, wiped and sliced
1 onion, diced
$\frac{1}{4}$ cup quick-cooking barley
$\frac{1}{2}$ teaspoon cumin
salt and pepper to taste
dash Worcestershire sauce

Simmer the leg in a 5-quart soup pot in 6 to 8 cups of water or chicken stock for 4 hours. Strain. Return the broth to the kettle and remove and chop the meat. Combine the meat and the remaining ingredients with the stock and simmer 1 hour until the vegetables are tender, adding more stock if necessary.

Makes about 2 quarts.

Winter Vegetable Soup

Because winter is a long season in Maine, root vegetables are an important part of our diet. When we first began making this soup, we had to use frozen peas or green beans for a touch of green. Now fresh green veggies are available all year. Since you need so few to get that extra verdant dimension, we suggest you make the modest investment. The vegetables listed are ones we can usually find in our refrigerator. Add or subtract at will. This is a meal!

1 cup onion, finely chopped
1 large clove garlic, minced
1 cup celery, diced
2 tablespoons vegetable oil
1 large beefy soup bone
6 cups beef broth, canned or homemade
2 medium carrots, cut in rounds
1 white turnip, diced
1 cup rutabaga, diced
1 cup canned tomatoes, chopped, with juice
1 cup red potatoes, diced coarsely, skins on
1 cup cabbage, coarsely chopped
¼ cup quick-cooking barley
½ cup green beans cut into 2-inch pieces (optional)
¼ cup fresh or frozen peas (optional)
salt and pepper to taste

In a large soup pot, sauté the onion, garlic, and celery in oil until soft. Trim all fat off the soup bone, place it in the pot, and cover with the beef broth. Add the carrots, turnip, rutabaga, and tomatoes and simmer 1 to 2 hours or until the meat is tender. Add the rest of the ingredients and simmer for ½ hour more. Cool the soup. Remove the meat from the bone and dice it up, returning it to the pot. When the soup has cooled, skim the fat from the top, add the salt and pepper, and serve.

Serves 6 to 8.

※ ※ ※

A tourist came to a fork in the road. Each road had a sign to Portland. The tourist spied a fisherman repairing nets in his front yard. He rolled down his window and hollered, "Make any difference which road I take to Portland?"

Without glancing up, the fisherman said, "Not to me it don't."

Onion and Bean Chowder

A baked bean picnic supper after the 4th of July parade is an event everyone looks forward to. What to do 5 days later with the last of the beans is another matter! Here's one solution.

2 cups onions, finely chopped
3 tablespoons chicken fat or vegetable oil
1 cup baked beans
3 cups potatoes, diced or thinly sliced
salt and pepper to taste
1 teaspoon thyme
1 teaspoon parsley, chopped
4 cups hot milk

Sauté the onions in fat or oil over low heat until soft, stirring often. Add the beans, potatoes, and seasonings, including the parsley, with just enough water to cook the potatoes. When the potatoes are tender, add the milk and bring just to a simmer, then serve.

Serves 6.

Split Pea Soup

This is such a simple soup, yet its flavor can best be described as contentment in a bowl.

½ pound green or yellow split peas
4 cups chicken stock or water
1 ham hock, smoked or not
⅓ cup onions, chopped
⅓ cup celery, chopped
⅓ cup carrots, diced
1 small bay leaf

Wash and drain the split peas. Combine all the ingredients in a soup kettle with a tight-fitting lid. Bring to a boil. Reduce the heat and simmer, covered, for 2 hours, stirring occasionally. Remove the ham hock and cool slightly. Cut the ham off the bone and dice before returning it to the soup. Heat thoroughly and remove the bay leaf before serving. If you want a thicker soup, puree ½ of it in a blender.

Serves 4.

Shinbone Soup

An aromatic, hearty soup, fiber-filled and fragrant. The kind of soup you love to know is waiting at the end of a day of skating on the pond.

1 cracked shinbone (ask the butcher to do it)
4 quarts water (to start with)
1 bay leaf
1 cup cabbage, chopped
4 cups diced vegetables (potatoes, onions, celery, carrots,
        parsnips, turnip, etc.)
½ cup pearl barley, rinsed
salt and pepper to taste
1 tablespoon parsley, chopped

Simmer the shinbone in the water with the bay leaf until the marrow is dissolved and the meat separates from the bone. About 1½ hours before serving, remove the bay leaf and add the vegetables and barley to thicken. Season with the salt and pepper. If your soup is too thick, reduce it with boiling water. Sprinkle with the chopped parsley and serve in large bowls with thick, crusty bread.

Serves 6 to 8.

Two Pea Soup

A lovely summer soup, good hot or cold. A nice accompaniment is open-faced cream cheese and smoked salmon sandwiches.

3 tablespoons vegetable oil
1 large onion, chopped
2 celery stalks, chopped
2 carrots, grated or chopped
3 or 4 cloves of garlic, minced
½ teaspoon thyme
½ pound dried split peas, rinsed
4 cups chicken stock
1 bay leaf
2 cups water
1½ cups frozen peas, thawed

In a soup kettle, heat the oil and cook the onion, celery, carrots, garlic, and thyme, covered, over medium-low heat, stirring often, for 10 minutes. Add the split peas, stock, bay leaf, and water. Bring to a boil, skimming the froth. Cook the soup, partially covered, for 1 hour. Discard the bay leaf. In a blender mix the soup in batches, return it to the pot, add the peas, and heat through. Thin the soup as desired with hot water or milk.

Serves 6 to 8.

Peter Cohen's Famous Emergency-Supper Soup

Sally's husband, Peter, invented this miracle one evening when Sally was wrestling with her new computer to finish this book, and the computer was winning. This soup is so good we hope everyone will keep the ingredients on hand. It cooks in no time and is a complete meal.

1 48-ounce can chicken broth
½ can water
2 whole boneless, skinless chicken breasts (4 halves)
1 16-ounce can peeled whole tomatoes
1 16-ounce can artichoke hearts (*not* in marinade)

Empty the can of chicken broth and the ½ can of water into a large saucepan. Cut the chicken breasts into thin strips and add to the broth. Cut the tomatoes into thin strips and add to the pot. Cut about ⅔ of the artichokes into bite-size pieces and add them, as well as the liquid from the can. Reserve a couple of the artichoke hearts for the salad that goes with the soup. Simmer the soup for about 15 minutes and serve hot, with a tossed green salad and warm French bread.

Serves 6.

Sweet Potato Soup

This probably originated in some place like Jamaica, but it has
a lovely creamy personality that our neighbors seem to like.
Elegant served cold in the summer, too.

1½ pounds sweet potatoes, peeled and cut into chunks
2 tablespoons canola oil
1 large onion, chopped
1 carrot, peeled and sliced
2 ribs celery, diced
6 cups chicken stock
1 tablespoon frozen orange juice concentrate
pinch grated fresh nutmeg
salt and white pepper to taste
¼ cup plain lowfat yogurt

Boil the sweet potatoes until tender. Meanwhile, pour the
oil into a heavy 5-quart saucepan and sauté the onion,
carrot, and celery until the onion is soft. Mash the sweet
potatoes and put them in the pot with the sautéed vegetables. Add the chicken stock, orange juice concentrate, nutmeg, salt, and pepper. Puree for 5 or 6 seconds in a blender
or food processer. Reheat and stir in the yogurt or serve a
spoonful on top of each cup of the soup.

Serves 4 to 6.

Cream of Parsnip Soup

Parsnips are a creamy, sweet root vegetable that has been given a bad rap, kind of like turnips. They are used a lot in Maine because until recently they were one of the few fresh vegetables available all winter long. This lovely soup reminds us of Sunday dinner at Mom's.

2 tablespoons canola oil
1 large carrot, peeled and finely diced
1 large onion, peeled and diced small
3 parsnips (or 2 large), peeled and finely diced
2 cloves garlic, peeled and finely diced
1 russet potato, peeled and diced
¼ cup fresh parsley, chopped
1 teaspoon dried tarragon
pinch fresh nutmeg, grated
4 cups chicken stock
salt and white pepper to taste
½ cup half-and-half

Pour the canola oil into the bottom of a heavy, deep enameled iron pot or stovetop-safe casserole. Add the carrot, onion, parsnips, and garlic. Sauté until the vegetables are soft, about 5 minutes, stirring frequently. Add the potato, parsley, tarragon, nutmeg, and stock. Cover and simmer for about 20 minutes to ½ hour, until everything is very tender. Put through a blender in batches and then return to the pot. Add the salt, pepper, and half-and-half. Reheat but do not boil. If desired, you may leave a cup or so of the soup unblended.

Serves 4 to 6.

Beef Borscht

Terry was born in Russia but was raised in Shanghai, China, from the time she was four. Borscht, a soup that was a staple in her family's home, was superbly prepared by their Chinese cook, Ivan—so called because he worked for a Russian family. Borscht is a true meal in a bowl.

1½ quarts water
2 pounds beef soup bone, cracked, with lots of meat attached
2 cups tomato juice
1 large onion, peeled and diced
1 teaspoon salt
2 cups beets, grated
2 cup carrots, grated
3 cups cabbage, grated
1 cup potato, diced, skins on
1 clove garlic, minced
1 teaspoon sugar
1 tablespoon vinegar
2 teaspoons fresh dill weed or 1 teaspoon dried
sour cream

In 1 quart of the water, boil the beef bones for 1½ hours, skimming any foam that forms. Remove the beef from the bones and cut into pieces. Return the meat to the broth. Add the tomato juice, vegetables, and remaining ½ quart of water and simmer for another ½ hour. Add the sugar, vinegar, and dill weed and serve piping hot in large bowls with a dollop of sour cream in each bowl of soup.

Serves 6.

Rice, Grains, Pasta, and Potatoes

Although Mainers tend to stick to the basics when cooking rice, grains, pasta, and potatoes, they are becoming more aware of the many possibilities of these wholesome and delicious foods. In addition to some of the unadorned recipes that Mainers have always loved, we offer you a few simple variations that go well with the extraordinary seafood and game that are so plentiful here.

Garlic Mashed Potatoes

Potatoes are a huge part of our state's economy. Sometimes school openings are adjusted so that kids can help their parents with the harvest. We've been glad to note recently that some of the nation's leading restaurants have begun to leave the peelings on their potatoes, even when they mash them. Since that's where so many of the nutrients are, we hope you'll try it. Tastes just fine, too. In the summer, when fresh chives abound, we cut some up and add to the mix (or mash).

1 pound russet potatoes, peeled or not, as you like
2 tablespoons butter or margarine
2 cloves garlic, crushed
salt and ground white pepper to taste
$\frac{1}{4}$ to $\frac{1}{3}$ cup hot milk

Cut the potatoes into 2-inch cubes and boil until very tender and soft. Drain. Add the butter, garlic, salt, pepper, and about $\frac{1}{8}$ cup of the milk. With a hand mixer, beat the potatoes until there are no lumps. Add just enough more milk to reach the desired degree of fluffiness. Serve piping hot.

Serves 4 to 6.

Herbed Potatoes in Olive Oil

2½ pounds russet potatoes, scrubbed and sliced ¼-inch
    thick, skins on
⅔ cup olive oil
2 cloves garlic, crushed
1 tablespoon dried oregano
1 tablespoon dried basil
2 tablespoons fresh parsley, minced
¼ teaspoon cayenne pepper
salt to taste (optional)

After slicing the potatoes, cover them in cold water and set
aside. Combine the rest of the ingredients in a large bowl.
Drain the potatoes and pat dry. Add the potatoes to the
bowl, turning them to coat well with the oil mixture.
Spread in a 12- by 14-inch baking dish or foil-lined cookie
sheet. Bake in a 375° oven until edges are golden brown,
about 45 minutes to 1 hour.

Serves 4.

Candied Sweet Potatoes

Boy oh boy, this one is wicked good! Make these at Thanksgiving and Christmas for sure, and they're great with your Easter ham as well.

3 to 4 pounds sweet potatoes
3 to 4 tablespoons butter
½ cup dark brown sugar
3 tablespoons frozen orange juice
1 teaspoon grated orange zest
⅛ cup curaçao (or other orange liqueur)
⅛ cup chicken stock

Peel the sweet potatoes and quarter them. Place the potatoes in a large saucepan, cover with cold water, and simmer for 15 to 20 minutes, or until they are barely tender. Melt the butter in a skillet and add the brown sugar, orange juice, orange zest, curaçao, and chicken stock. Simmer 10 to 15 minutes, stirring occasionally, until the mixture is slightly reduced and a little thickened. Place the sweet potatoes in a casserole, pour the syrup over the top, and bake at 350° for about 20 to 25 minutes, basting occasionally.

Serves 8.

Sweet Potatoes with Cider and Brown Sugar

4 pounds sweet potatoes, peeled and diced into 1-inch
    cubes
2½ cups apple cider
½ cup dark brown sugar
1 stick butter or margarine
2-inch piece cinnamon stick
3 Granny Smith apples, peeled and cubed

In a large stainless steel saucepan, combine all the ingredients except ¼ of the stick of butter and the apples. Simmer, partially uncovered, until tender, about 30 minutes.
While the potatoes are cooking, sauté the apples in the rest
of the butter until they are soft but not mushy. Cool the
potatoes slightly and remove the cinnamon stick. Puree the
potatoes in a food processor. Place the potatoes in an oven-
proof casserole and carefully stir in the apples. Cover and
bake in a preheated 350° oven until warm, about 20 to
25 minutes.

Serves 4 to 6.

Hot Potato Salad

We suspect this recipe may have moved to Maine "from away," possibly from Pennsylvania. No matter; Mainers have made it their own.

6 medium potatoes
2 hard-boiled eggs, chopped
4 slices bacon, diced
¼ cup onion, minced
1 egg, beaten
¼ cup cider vinegar
1¾ teaspoons salt

Cook the potatoes, cool, and slice or cut into ½-inch cubes. Add the chopped eggs. Fry the bacon and onion until the onion is a delicate brown and the bacon has begun to crisp. Drain, reserving the bacon fat. Add the fat slowly to the beaten egg and mix well. Add the vinegar and salt and pour the mixture over the potatoes. Add the bacon and onion. Mix lightly to blend well and heat in a double boiler. Serve hot.

Serves 6.

New Potatoes with Butter and Dill

It is impossible to describe the difference in taste between a new potato and a mature potato, but happily new potatoes are easy to pick out because they are so small and are found in the spring and early part of the summer. Really, they are baby potatoes and, like all baby vegetables, are sweet and tender. If they are not firm, don't buy them. We boil them, and they don't want to cook a long time. The tinier the better, so look for ones no larger than a golf ball. If you see any the size of marbles, lucky you!

1 to 1½ pounds new white or red potatoes
salt (optional)
1 to 2 tablespoons butter
1 tablespoon fresh dill, rinsed, dried, and minced

Scrub the potatoes but leave the skins on. Four-star restaurants peel a narrow band right around the potato's mid section, but we gave that up long ago as being too time-consuming and unnecessary. Put the potatoes in a bit of water in a saucepan, add a pinch of salt if desired, and boil until just tender, from 2 to 6 minutes or so. Drain and add the butter. Shake the pan gently to coat all the potatoes, place them in a warm serving bowl, and sprinkle with the dill. Add a bit more salt if desired. Serve at once.

Serves 4 to 6.

Brown Rice à l'Orange

Don't be intimidated by the title. Basically, you just cook the rice in orange juice. You don't have to use brown rice, either; you can use white or part wild rice as well. If you'd like to turn this into a pilaf, add ¹/₂ cup celery, diced, and ¹/₂ cup onion, diced, both lightly sautéed in a tablespoon of butter. The following is the basic master recipe. White rice will cook in 18 to 20 minutes, and we prefer chicken broth to beef broth for white rice.

1 cup brown rice
1¹/₄ cups beef broth
1 cup fresh orange juice
1 teaspoon grated orange rind
¹/₂ cup pecans, coarsely chopped
pinch of salt (optional)

Combine the above ingredients and cook, covered, for 45 minutes.

Serves 4.

Bulgur with Mushroom Sauce

Bulgur is cracked wheat that is hulled, steamed, and dried. It has a wonderful, nutty flavor that is not only good steeped in boiling water and served as you would rice, but mouth-watering when paired with an infinite variety of other favorite things, as in the following casserole.

1 tablespoon salt
2 cups water
1½ cups bulgur

Add the salt to the water and bring to a boil. Add the bulgur and let stand for ½ hour. Drain.

Mushroom Sauce

6 tablespoons olive oil
1 large onion, chopped
½ pound mushrooms, sliced
3 cloves garlic, finely minced
2 teaspoons parsley, finely minced
2 tablespoons ground cumin

Heat the olive oil in a skillet and sauté the onion, mushrooms, and garlic until limp. Add the parsley and sauté briefly. Add the cumin. Place the drained bulgur in a casserole or serving dish, add the sauce, and mix thoroughly. Serve, or let marinate for a while and reheat.

Serves 4.

Baked Pearl Barley

Barley is such a deeply satisfying dish, full of flavor and texture. Use it instead of noodles or rice, or even in place of potatoes.

2 or 3 scallions
½ pound mushrooms, wiped and sliced
2 tablespoons butter
3 cups chicken stock
½ teaspoon cumin
¾ cup quick-cooking pearl barley

Sauté the scallions and mushrooms in the butter until soft. Place them in the bottom of a heavy casserole. Add the stock, cumin, and barley. Bake, covered, in a preheated 325° oven, until the barley is tender, about 45 minutes.

Serves 4.

✾ ✾ ✾

Uncle Eben was always on the go—walking here and there. One time someone stopped to pick him up, and he said, "Oh, I'm in too much of a hurry, dear. Don't have time for a ride!"

From A Lobster in Every Pot

Macaroni and Cheese

*The comfort food from everyone's childhood, this casserole is as
popular in Maine as it is in the rest of the country. Add 4 turkey
hot dogs, and you have a hearty dinner.*

3 tablespoons butter or margarine
3 tablespoons flour
1 cup milk
1 cup sharp Cheddar cheese, plus ¼ cup for topping,
     grated
⅛ teaspoon salt, or to taste
⅛ teaspoon cayenne pepper
1 pound elbow macaroni, cooked and drained
½ cup white bread crumbs (optional)
sprinkling of paprika

Melt the butter in a 2-quart saucepan and add the flour,
stirring with a wire whisk. Whisk over low heat for
1 minute, then slowly add the milk, whisking until it
thickens. Add 1 cup of the grated cheese and stir until the
cheese is melted. Add the salt and cayenne pepper.
     Put the macaroni in a casserole and pour the cheese
sauce on top. Sprinkle the bread crumbs on top, if desired.
Sprinkle the last of the cheese over all, and top with a
sprinkling of paprika. Bake in a 350° oven for 45 minutes,
or until heated through and the cheese is melted and
golden brown.

Serves 4 to 6.

Salmon Noodles Alfredo

We love the new, fresh, ready-to-serve pasta sauces now available in most supermarkets. One of the big treats about living in Maine is the availability of fresh, affordable salmon all year long. When time is a factor, this recipe is a godsend. It's also a dish gracious enough for a company dinner.

6 ounces medium-wide egg noodles
1 10-ounce container fresh Alfredo sauce
3 to 4 ounces milk
1 cup frozen peas
¾ pound cooked, boned salmon

Cook the noodles in 3 quarts of boiling salted water until barely tender. Drain and set aside. Heat the Alfredo sauce with the milk, starting with 3 ounces of milk and adding more if a thinner consistency is desired. Add the noodles to the sauce. Add the peas to the noodle mixture. Finally, gently flake the salmon into the noodles and sauce, and pour into a 3-quart casserole. Heat gently and serve.

Chicken works well with this recipe, too. If you are serving from the kitchen, you may serve the Noodles Alfredo right from the pan. Using the casserole allows you to prepare it earlier in the day.

Serves 4.

Scalloped Potatoes

If you're looking for a hearty, scrumptious, easy time-saver, this potato recipe is for you. Great with broiled fish, wonderful with meatloaf, and if you have any baked ham scraps or the morning's leftover bacon crumbs, layer them in as well, and you have a main course. Just add a salad.

4 large russet potatoes, thinly sliced
1 large onion, very thinly sliced
1 cup Cheddar cheese, grated
salt and freshly ground pepper to taste
1½ cups light cream
sprinkling of paprika

Spray a 2-quart casserole or rectangular baking dish with vegetable spray. Layer ½ the potatoes in the bottom of the dish. Layer ½ of the onions on top of the potatoes and follow with ½ of the cheese. Add salt and pepper. Repeat with the rest of the potatoes, onions, and cheese. Salt and pepper again and pour the cream over all. Sprinkle some paprika on top and bake in a preheated 350° oven for approximately 1 hour or until the potatoes are tender.

Serves 4 to 6.

Baked Couscous Casserole

Couscous is a marvelous semolina product that is almost always packaged precooked. It is a traditional dish of the North African countries, often served with fish, chicken, and lamb stews. But it can stand on its own as a side dish. Add whatever vegetables you love best.

2 tablespoons olive oil
1 medium onion, chopped
1 large clove garlic, minced
1 large tomato, diced (or 1 cup canned tomatoes, diced, plus ¼ cup juice)
1 large carrot, diced small
1 cup couscous
½ teaspoon cumin
1 tablespoon parsley, chopped
2 cups chicken stock (2½ cups if you use fresh tomato)

In a 2-quart heavy, enameled baking dish, sauté the onion, garlic, tomato, and carrot in the oil for 4 or 5 minutes over low heat, stirring frequently. Add the couscous, seasonings, and chicken stock and bring to a boil. Remove from the heat, cover, and place in a preheated 325° oven for 10 to 12 minutes. Fluff with a fork before serving.

Serves 4.

Twice-Baked Potatoes

Shades of our childhood! And these taste just as good as you remember.

3 large russet potatoes, scrubbed
2 tablespoons butter
1 cup sharp Cheddar cheese, grated
½ cup sour cream
3 tablespoons fresh chives, chopped
salt and white pepper to taste

Scrub the potatoes and prick them in 2 or 3 places. Place them on a cookie sheet and bake in a preheated 400° oven until they are tender, about 1 hour. Cut each potato in half lengthwise. Scoop out the centers very carefully and put them in a bowl with the butter. Reserve the potato jackets and place them back on the cookie sheet.

Mash the potatoes until they are fluffy. Mix in the cheese, sour cream, chives, and salt and pepper. Mound the potato mixture back into the shells, return them to the oven, and bake for an additional 15 to 20 minutes.

Serves 6.

Linguine with Mussels

Many people who live on the shore Down East have mussel beds in their front yards. There are lots and lots of ways to cook these shiny black-shelled mollusks; but certainly one of the most intriguing is to pretend they are clams (they are close cousins, in fact) and serve them in the Italian fashion, with linguine. You won't regret it. This one's for a crowd.

2½ quarts mussels in shells (about 75)
2 cloves garlic, finely minced
2 onions, thinly sliced
¼ cup olive oil
2 lemons, thinly sliced
2 large cans (1 pound 13 ounces each) crushed Italian
     tomatoes
6 ounces tomato paste
2 teaspoons dried basil
1½ tablespoons oregano
1½ teaspoons salt
⅛ teaspoon red pepper flakes
½ teaspoon black pepper
2 cups red wine
2 pounds linguine

Scrub and de-beard the mussels (pull off the little clumps of threadlike material clinging to the shells). Sauté the garlic and onion in the oil in a 6-quart kettle. When the onion is golden and soft, add the lemon slices, tomatoes, tomato paste, basil, oregano, salt, and peppers. Cover and simmer over low heat for 25 minutes. Add the wine and simmer uncovered until the sauce thickens, about 15 to

20 minutes. The sauce may be prepared in advance up
until this point—the addition of the mussels.

Finally, add the mussels to the sauce, cover, and cook
over medium-high heat until the mussels open, approximately 5 minutes. Cook the linguine in another large pot
according to the package directions. Drain and toss with a
couple of tablespoons of olive oil to prevent the strands
from sticking. Place the linguine in a very large, shallow
bowl and pour the cooked mussels and tomato sauce over
the top. Serve immediately.

Serves 8 to 10.

❋ ❋ ❋

*Fishermen used to believe if they wanted some wind,
they'd throw a coin in the water. Well, Grover Merchant
wanted wind, so he threw a nickel in. Instead of asking
for a couple of pennies' worth, he asked for a nickel's
worth—and he got drowned right out there!
A nickel could buy a lot more in those days!*

From A Lobster in Every Pot

Seafood

Along with The Rocky Coast, Wry Humor, and Moose, Seafood is right up there in the list of things that come to mind when you hear the word "Maine." Lobsters are our most famous seafood; but the tiny, sweet shrimp that appear in the late winter and early spring, the beds of glistening black mussels that line the shore along with the clams hiding in the mud, the cod, salmon, bluefish, mackerel, and trout—these and so many more make seafood cookery in Maine one of life's most creative and rewarding culinary experiences. Now that most everything caught and trapped in the state is available fresh all over the country, you too can enjoy our seafood.

Shrimp Wiggle

Yes, that's really its name; and no, we don't know why. It always turns up at the covered dish supper at the church and is one of the most popular dishes. It's a Maine "comfort food."

2 pounds Maine shrimp, shelled (you don't have to devein
      Maine shrimp)
1 cup white sauce
1 large can French peas (the tiny ones), drained
4 tablespoons butter
1 teaspoon onion juice or grated fresh onion
dash of salt and pepper
dash of cayenne pepper, if so inclined
2 hard-boiled eggs, diced
2 tablespoons minced parsley

Cook the shrimp in hot water to cover for not more than
2 minutes. Drain and mix with the white sauce. Combine
the peas, butter, and all other ingredients, except eggs and
parsley, with the creamed shrimp. Serve over toast, in patty
shells, or over biscuits, garnished with hard-boiled eggs
and parsley.

Serves 6.

Shrimp Neptune

This elegant recipe may easily be doubled, kept warm in a chafing dish, and served at a buffet.

2 tablespoons butter or margarine
1 tablespoon scallions, minced
¼ pound mushrooms, wiped and sliced
1 can frozen or canned cream of shrimp soup (½ cup
    whole milk added if condensed)
1 cup light sour cream
½ teaspoon Worcestershire sauce
¼ teaspoon ground white pepper
2 pounds cooked shrimp (first peeled and deveined)
3 tablespoons sherry

Melt the butter in a large skillet and sauté the scallions and mushrooms over medium heat until wilted. Add the soup, sour cream, Worcestershire sauce, and pepper and stir over low heat until smooth. Do not allow the sauce to boil. Stir in the shrimp and sherry and heat through. Serve over rice.

Serves 6.

Shrimp Greco

We don't know why feta cheese, that great Greek invention, does such wonderful things for shrimp, but who cares? A great party dish, it can be prepared beforehand up to adding the shrimp— even a day before. Then reheat, add cleaned shrimp and cheese, and voilà!

2 pounds raw shrimp
2 cloves garlic, minced
1 small onion, chopped
¼ cup olive oil
¼ cup dry vermouth
2 cups canned crushed tomatoes
1 tablespoon tomato paste
2 teaspoons dried oregano
2 teaspoons dried basil
dash of Tabasco
pinch of salt, if desired (but feta is very salty)
freshly ground black pepper to taste
½ pound feta cheese, cut into small chunks

Shell and devein the shrimp. Sauté the garlic and onion in olive oil until they are limp. Add the vermouth and simmer 2 or 3 minutes to reduce. Add the tomatoes, tomato paste, oregano, basil, and Tabasco and simmer for 10 minutes.

Add salt, if desired, and the pepper. Add the shrimp to the sauce and continue cooking for 3 to 4 minutes or until they turn pink. Add the cut-up feta cheese. Cook until the shrimp are done and the cheese is heated through but not completely melted. Serve with rice.

Serves 4 to 6.

❋ ❋ ❋

Some definitions of Maine words and phrases

Spleeny: At odds with the world; not too comfortable in one's skin. "Malaise-ish"—could feel better.

Numb: Slow on the uptake—definitely not bright.

Dear (pronounced dee-ah): Common form of address; father addressing son—clam digger to packer— love has nothing to do with it.

Ayeh: Yes or uh-huh or of course. Definitely affirmative. But only Mainers can say it while inhaling not aspirating.

Toe injection: The front of the boot projected at the derrier.

Thicker'n spatters: Bountiful. Surfeit of too much; more than enough.

Summer mahogany: The fancy boats and the people "from away" who own them.

Peaked: (pronounced pee-kid): Weak, pale, not quite up to snuff.

Folks "from away": ANYONE who comes from ANYWHERE beyond Maine's borders.

Broiled Barbecued Shrimp

This is a recipe Terry brought with her from her former home-town of New Orleans, and everybody she knows is certainly glad she did.

1 cup olive oil
½ teaspoon salt
3 tablespoons parsley, chopped
1 tablespoon basil
2 cloves garlic, minced
1 tablespoon tomato sauce or chili sauce
1 teaspoon freshly ground pepper
1 tablespoon wine vinegar
2 pounds shrimp, shelled and deveined, with tails on

Make a sauce by mixing all the ingredients except the shrimp. Arrange the shrimp in a shallow pan, 9 by 14 inches, and pour the sauce over them. Marinate for several hours. Broil for 4 to 8 minutes. Arrange the shrimp on a warm serving dish or serve them in the broiling pan. You eat them by picking them up by the tails and dipping them into the hot sauce, so plates and plenty of paper napkins are needed.

Serves 6.

Shrimp and Corn Sauté

We're always on the lookout for ways to save time, and the corn and peppers in this shrimp recipe are a creative way to combine fish and vegetables. Corn bread and a salad go well with this.

1 green pepper, finely chopped
4 tablespoons butter or margarine
1½ cups corn kernels
1½ cups shelled cooked shrimp
½ cup heavy cream
salt and pepper to taste
dash paprika

Sauté the green pepper in the butter. Add the corn and let it heat thoroughly. Add the shrimp and the cream and mix well. Cover the pan and simmer for 3 or 4 minutes. Season to taste with salt, freshly ground black pepper, and paprika.

Serves 4 to 6.

✖ ✖ ✖

Every American child knows that we have the Indians to thank for corn. But every Mainer knows that the sooner you get it out of the field and into the pot the better. We have known Mainers to have a pot of water boiling in the field.

Boiled or Steamed Lobster

Did you know that lobsters are cannibals? There are at least two chambers in each lobster pot (or trap) so that one lobster won't eat the other if two are caught.

In France lobsters have become the traditional Christmas dinner, and the week before Christmas there are large cargo planes at the Bangor airport loading them up for their trip to Paris.

*When you have lobsters for dinner, wear your old clothes, have plenty of paper napkins handy, put a large bowl in the center of the table for the pieces of shell, and melt lots of butter for dipping. There are those who say "boil 'em" and there are those who say "steam 'em." We've tried both, and there's no difference in taste. In Maine we often use seawater, with some seaweed added to our lobster kettle. If you want your shore dinner to be **really** traditional, serve your lobster with garlic bread, a big salad, corn on the cob, and wild blueberry pie. And don't forget nutcrackers to break the shells and picks to get all the tender meat out. A sharp knife for slitting the underside of the body is a help, too.*

4 1½-pound lobsters
seawater if you can get it
¼ pound butter, melted
fresh lemon juice (optional)

If you are steaming the lobsters, pour 1 to 2 inches of water in the bottom of a very large pot or canning-size kettle. When the water is boiling rapidly, plunge the lobsters head first into the pot. Place the top on immediately and steam for 10 to 15 minutes.

If you are boiling, fill the pot ⅔ full of water and bring to a boil. Plunge the lobsters in head first, return to a boil, and boil for 18 to 20 minutes.

Drain and cut the rubber bands from the claws. Serve with individual cups of the melted butter and, if desired, with the lemon juice.

Serves 4.

Maine Lobster Stew

Beware! This is not a diet meal! However, once or twice a year it is good for the soul to throw caution to the winds, and this, my dears, is Down East soul food at its most sublime.

6 tablespoons butter
2½ cups cooked lobster meat
1 pint Lobster Bouillon
1 quart milk, scalded
2 egg yolks
1 cup cream
salt and freshly ground pepper to taste
sprinkling of paprika

Melt the butter in a large saucepan, add the lobster meat, and toss for several minutes to brown lightly. Add the bouillon and milk and let it heat through. Beat the egg yolks with the cream, stir into the bouillon mixture, and continue stirring until the stew is very hot. Season with the salt and pepper. Serve in large bowls with a sprinkling of paprika. Pilot (oyster) crackers are the traditional accompaniment, but good crusty French bread is practically perfect.

Serves 6.

Lobster Bouillon

leftover lobster shells
1 cup water that lobster was cooked in
½ cup white wine
1 cup chicken broth
1 small onion, halved
1 small carrot, sliced

Crush the lobster shells. Place them with the rest of the
ingredients in a large pot and simmer for 15 minutes.
Discard the shells and put the liquid through a fine strainer.

Makes 2 cups.

❈ ❈ ❈

*To watch a Mainer consume a lobster is to see "waste not"
in action—first the claws, then the body, then with much
sucking, all the meat and juice out of each leg, then the
head. And finally the shells are dumped into the compost.*

Lobster Fra Diavolo

Our variation on the classic theme uses apple brandy (Calvados). There's nothing really difficult about the preparation, but it does take a bit of time, especially the first go-round. Once you get used to dealing with large pieces of lobster, you're home free. Serve with rice cooked in chicken broth and seasoned with 1/2 teaspoon cumin. It's a show-stopper.

2 lobsters (1 to 1½ pounds each)
4 tablespoons virgin olive oil
¼ cup parsley, chopped
2 teaspoons cumin powder
1 small onion, finely diced
1 clove garlic, minced
pinch of ground cloves
pinch of ground mace
salt and white pepper to taste
2 cups canned crushed tomatoes
¼ cup Calvados or other apple brandy

Plunge the lobsters into a large pot of boiling water for 1 minute to kill them. Remove from the pot and split lengthwise down the center. Heat the oil in a large skillet and cook the lobsters in the oil for about 10 minutes. Add the parsley, cumin, onion, garlic, seasonings, and tomatoes. Cover and cook 10 minutes longer, stirring often. Arrange the lobster halves on a large oval platter and spoon the rice around them. Pour the brandy over the lobster and light it just before serving.

Serves 4.

Maine Lobster Casserole

This old Maine recipe has been around for generations. In addi-
tion to its wonderful flavor, it has several other great attributes.
It calls for the use of "chicken lobsters," which are the smaller,
less expensive, one-pounders. It is a hearty casserole and can be
put together and refrigerated until an hour or so before heating.

2 tablespoons butter
2 tablespoons flour
½ teaspoon dry mustard
salt and paprika to taste
1 cup half-and-half
½ cup whole milk
4 or 5 drops Worcestershire sauce
5 slices white bread, crusts removed, cut into 1-inch cubes
3 chicken lobsters, boiled and meat removed
½ cup crushed corn flakes

Melt the butter in the top of a double boiler. Add the flour,
mustard, salt, paprika, and Worcestershire sauce. After
making a paste of these, slowly add the half-and-half, and
the whole milk. Stir constantly with a wire whisk to make
smooth and continue to cook until thickened. Add the
bread cubes and the lobster meat, cut into bite-size pieces.
Mix well and pour into a casserole. Top the mixture with
the crushed corn flakes. Bake in a preheated 350° oven only
long enough to heat through and lightly toast the topping.

You may refrigerate before baking. If you do, bring out
of the refrigerator at least 1 hour before baking.

Serves 4.

Maine's Own Lobster Roll

2 cups chilled cooked lobster meat
2 tablespoons mayonnaise
¼ cup celery, finely diced
4 hamburger rolls, split and toasted
4 tablespoons butter, melted

Blend together the lobster meat, mayonnaise, and celery.
Mix well and refrigerate until ready to use. Split and toast
the rolls and brush with the melted butter. Fill the rolls
with the lobster mixture.

Serves 4.

✖ ✖ ✖

*Chowder, from the French "la chaudiere," came to Maine
via neighbor Nova Scotia. Chowder* must *have milk or
cream, potatoes, and seafood, but* never *tomatoes. The
Maine legislature once introduced a bill to outlaw forever
the mixing of clams and tomatoes.*

Omelet with Lobster

When you come from the lobster capital of the world, you tend to get reckless. Lobster for breakfast? What the hey . . . why not?

1 cup thin white sauce
1 cup cooked lobster meat in chunks
salt and pepper to taste
4 egg yolks, beaten
⅓ cup milk
4 egg whites, beaten stiff
2 tablespoons butter

Put the white sauce in the top of a double boiler, add the lobster meat to it, and season with the salt and pepper. Blend the yolks with the milk, fold in the whites, and fold the lobster mixture into the egg mixture. Melt the butter in a large frying pan and cook the omelet until the bottom begins to brown and the mixture begins to puff. Finish cooking in a preheated 400° oven or under the broiler, until the top sets. Fold in half and serve at once.

Serves 4.

Salmon with Cream

4 salmon steaks
flour for dusting
4 tablespoons butter
salt and pepper to taste
⅓ cup sherry
1 cup heavy cream
beurre manié (2 tablespoons butter kneaded with
    3 tablespoons flour)
2 tablespoons parsley, chopped

Dust the steaks lightly with the flour and sauté them in the butter until nicely browned on both sides. Add salt and pepper. Cook the salmon 10 minutes for each inch of thickness and when they are done remove them to a hot platter. They should feel firm on both sides to a light touch with your finger.

Add the sherry to the pan and allow it to cook down for 1 or 2 minutes. Add the cream and the beurre manié and stir until it is nicely thickened. Add the chopped parsley, correct the seasoning, and pour the sauce over the salmon.

Serves 4.

Poached Salmon Steaks with Mustard Sauce

1 8-ounce bottle clam juice
½ cup white wine
1 celery stalk, chopped
1 small onion, halved
2 or 3 sprigs fresh thyme, if available
4 salmon steaks, 1½ inches thick

Put all the ingredients except the salmon steaks in a saucepan large enough to hold the 4 steaks in one layer, and simmer for 10 minutes. Pour through a strainer and return to the saucepan. Place the salmon in the liquid and add enough water to just cover the fish.

The rule for cooking fish is to cook for 10 minutes per inch of thickness, so simmer the steaks very gently for 15 minutes or until they feel firm when you press on them gently with your finger. If you press on them *before* you cook them, you will be able to tell the difference. Remove the fish with a slotted spatula and place on a warm serving platter. Serve with Mustard Sauce.

Serves 4.

Mustard Sauce

½ cup light mayonnaise
¼ cup light sour cream
1 teaspoon Dijon mustard

Mix the ingredients and heat very gently until warm.

Maine Salmon with Egg Sauce

6 to 8 cups water, lightly salted
2 bay leaves
2 tablespoons pickling spices
1 lemon, sliced
freshly ground black pepper
¼ cup parsley, chopped
sprinkling of paprika
4 to 6 medium salmon steaks (about 1¼ inches thick)

Place all the ingredients except the salmon in a fish poacher or a rectangular pan and boil for 15 minutes to combine the flavors. Lower the salmon steaks gently into the poaching liquor and simmer about 10 minutes or until the fish is firm to the touch. Drain and serve on a heated platter. Cover with Egg Sauce.

Serves 4 to 6.

Egg Sauce

⅓ stick butter, melted
3 tablespoons flour
1 cup fish stock or bottled clam juice
1 cup milk or cream
1 tablespoon prepared mustard
1 teaspoon powdered mustard
4 hard-boiled eggs, chopped
salt and pepper to taste

In a saucepan, melt the butter until bubbling. Add the flour and whisk to mix. Cook, whisking, for 1 to 2 minutes. Add the fish stock slowly, whisking constantly, and then add the milk or cream. Add the two mustards and continue whisking and heating slowly until it thickens. Stir in the eggs, salt, and pepper.

Serves 4 to 6.

Mussels in Béchamel Sauce

*Wild mussels are so plentiful here, you can go down to the shore
and collect enough in ten minutes at low tide to feed ten people.
Generally, they are steamed in white wine with 2 or 3 cloves
of chopped garlic, a few chopped shallots, and some chopped
parsley until they have opened up, from 5 to 10 minutes.
They're served in bowls with the liquid and with French bread
for dipping. But the following recipe is a slightly novel way to
cook mussels, and we love it.*

2 quarts of mussels, washed and debearded
2 cups water
1 cup white wine
1 onion, finely chopped
1 stalk celery, leaves left on
1 or 2 sprigs parsley
1½ cups Béchamel Sauce (recipe follows)
sprinkling of paprika
sprinkling of chopped parsley

Remove the clumps of threadlike material (beards) from
the mussel shells. Put the mussels in a large saucepan with
the 2 cups of water and the wine, onion, celery, and parsley. Cover and steam until the mussels open. Remove the
mussels from the shells and keep warm over hot water.

   Prepare Béchamel Sauce using some of the mussel
broth. Add the mussels. Serve in patty shells, over rice, on
mounds of mashed potatoes, or on toast triangles. Sprinkle
with the paprika and parsley.

Serves 4.

Béchamel Sauce

4 tablespoons butter
3 tablespoons flour
1¼ cups mussel broth
pinch paprika
salt and white pepper to taste

In a 2-quart saucepan, melt the butter. Add the flour and mix with a wire whisk over low heat for 1 minute. Slowly add the broth, whisking to keep lumps from forming. Whisk until the sauce has thickened, then add the paprika, salt, and pepper. Add mussels according to the preceding recipe.

Because of long cold winters, simple stick-to-the-ribs food is most popular, but exotic flavors are not strange to Mainers. Many a Maine sea captain took his whole family with him when he sailed to Spain, Africa, and the Caribbean.

Brandade de Morue or Baked Salt Codfish

1½ cups salt codfish (3 cups flaked)
4 garlic cloves, minced
1 cup extra-virgin olive oil
½ teaspoon Tabasco
freshly ground pepper to taste
1 cup heavy cream
1 cup mashed potatoes
toast triangles

Soak the codfish for 24 hours, changing water several times. Drain, cut into big chunks, and place in a sauce pot. Cover with cold water, bring to a simmer, and simmer gently for 1½ hours. Drain the fish, remove the skin and bones, and flake into small pieces. Reserve.

Place the garlic and olive oil in a blender and mix well. Add the codfish and blend. Blend in the Tabasco, pepper, and cream. Pour the mixture into a large bowl and add enough mashed potatoes (while beating by hand) to thicken it. If serving hot, bake in a 400° oven for 10 minutes and serve over the toast triangles. May also be served cold as an hors d'oeuvre on crackers.

It also makes a great breakfast dish. Shape the fish mixture into thick cakes, heat, perch a poached egg on top, and serve with crisp bacon.

Serves 6.

Salt Cod Soufflé

Salt was the preservative used to keep fish in the days before refrigeration. You'll need to soak or rinse the fish before beginning your recipe. It has a distinctive and wonderful flavor.

1 cup salt cod, shredded
1 cup milk
¼ cup butter
2 cups mashed potato
2 egg yolks, beaten
2 egg whites, beaten stiff
black pepper to taste

Shred, bone, and "freshen" the salt cod (rinse in cool water and squeeze water out). Place the cod in a saucepan with the milk and butter and heat till hot but not boiling. Add the potato and beat hard. Fold the beaten egg yolks into the beaten egg whites and mix gently until combined. Mix the eggs lightly into the fish-potato mixture, dust in a bit of pepper, and pour into a 1½-quart greased soufflé or baking dish. Bake for 30 minutes in a preheated 350° oven. It should come out high, light, and fluffy, a true soufflé. (See our remarks on soufflés under Cheese Soufflé.) Serve at once.

Serves 4.

New England Turkey or Baked Stuffed Cod with Mushroom Egg Sauce

During lean times, this wonderful dish has graced many a thrifty New England Thanksgiving table.

1 medium-size whole fish (4 to 7 pounds) or a large center
  cut of cod
2 cups (prepared) packaged stove-top stuffing
½ pound salt pork

Buy your fish cleaned and split open. Fill it with the stuffing. Sew up the opening or secure with toothpicks. Place the fish on an oiled baking dish covered with thin slices of the salt pork. Bake in a preheated 400° oven for 25 to 35 minutes, allowing 10 minutes per pound. Baste with pan juices during the baking. Remove to a hot platter, surround with plain boiled potatoes and green peas, and serve with the following egg sauce.

Serves 6 to 8.

Mushroom Egg Sauce

2 tablespoons butter
2 tablespoons flour
1 cup fish stock or clam juice
1 egg yolk, slightly beaten
¼ cup heavy cream
salt and pepper to taste
2 tablespoons white wine
½ cup sautéed mushrooms
1 tablespoon parsley, chopped

Melt the butter in a saucepan, whisk in the flour, and stir
for 1 minute. Slowly pour in the stock, whisking constantly.
Remove from the heat and add the egg yolk, cream, salt,
and pepper. Heat to just below a simmer, remove from the
heat, and add the wine, mushrooms, and parsley.

Serves 6 to 8.

Steamed Clams on Toast

*This is a terrific dish to serve for a brunch. It's served similarly
to onion soup, with toast in the bottom of the bowl.*

2 dozen clams, scrubbed
1 8-ounce bottle clam juice plus 2 cups water
½ stick butter
2 cloves garlic, finely chopped
4 tablespoons parsley, chopped
4 slices toasted bread (French or Italian are good);
     8 if slices are small
lemon wedges

In a large saucepan, steam the clams in the water and clam
juice. Remove the steamed clams from their shells. Check
the clam broth for salt and add some if needed. Melt the
butter with the garlic and add the parsley. Place 1 or
2 slices of bread in the bottom of each of 4 bowls, then
carefully divide the broth among the bowls. Serve at once
with the butter sauce and the wedges of lemon.

Serves 4.

Clam Hash

The cream in this hash dish makes it luscious. If you would like a lower-fat version, use half the amount of cheese and simply put a poached egg atop each portion.

6 tablespoons butter
1 tablespoon onion, finely minced
1½ cups cooked potatoes, in small cubes
2 cups minced clams
salt and pepper to taste
sprinkling of nutmeg
4 egg yolks
4 tablespoons grated Parmesan cheese
⅓ cup heavy cream

Melt the butter in a heavy skillet and cook the onion until it is just transparent. Add the cubed potatoes and the clams and press them down with a spatula. Salt and pepper lightly and add a sprinkling of nutmeg. Let the hash cook for about 10 minutes and stir with a fork or spatula, mixing in some of the crust that forms on the bottom. Press down again. Beat the yolks well and combine with the grated cheese and the cream. Pour very gently over the hash and cover tightly for a few minutes until the egg is set.

Serves 4.

Clam Soufflé

This has a lovely, piquant flavor. It is perfect on a warm summer evening with a fresh green salad and a loaf of herb bread.

1 cup clams, finely chopped
1 tablespoon lemon juice
1 cup milk
1 cup bottled clam juice
1 tablespoon Worcestershire sauce
4 tablespoons butter
4 tablespoons flour
salt and cayenne pepper to taste
2 egg whites, beaten stiff
1 cup cracker meal or crumbs

Sprinkle the clams with the lemon juice and let them stand while you make the cream sauce. Scald the milk and clam juice in the top of a double boiler. Add the Worcestershire sauce. Melt the butter and blend it with the flour. Add it to the clam juice and mix with a wire whisk until smooth. Add the clams to the sauce. Season with the salt and cayenne pepper, cook 3 minutes, and remove from the heat. Fold the stiffly beaten egg whites into the mixture. Pour into buttered individual ramekins; fill ⅔ full. Top with the cracker meal and dot with additional butter. Bake in a preheated 425° oven for 10 to 15 minutes.

Serves 4.

Baked Stuffed Sole

1 shallot, finely chopped
1/3 cup mushrooms, finely chopped
1 tablespoon oil
1 tablespoon butter
2 cups (prepared) stove-top stuffing
1 1/2 pounds fillet of sole
1/3 cup white wine
1/3 cup bottled clam juice
1/4 cup grated Parmesan cheese
beurre manié (2 tablespoons butter kneaded with
       2 tablespoons flour)
1/4 cup half-and-half or cream

Sauté the shallots and mushrooms in the oil and butter
until soft. Mix the prepared stuffing with the mushroom
mixture. Place about a heaping tablespoon (more or less
depending on the size of the fillets) in the middle of each
fillet, and roll the fillet around the stuffing.

Place these rolls, seam side down, in a lightly buttered
gratin or baking dish and carefully pour the wine and clam
juice around them. Sprinkle with the Parmesan cheese and
place in a preheated 450° oven. Bake for 15 to 20 minutes,
basting occasionally. Remove the juices from the pan, turn
the oven off, and return the pan to the oven to keep warm.
Add the beurre manié to the juice and whisk until it is
combined. Add the half-and-half or cream, pour over the
fish, and serve.

Serves 4.

Baked Stuffed Mackerel with Mustard Sauce

Mackerel has a strong flavor, so it needs robust ingredients in any cooking method. This recipe fills the bill.

2 medium onions, chopped
½ cup mushrooms, wiped and diced
1 clove garlic, minced
1 tablespoon canola oil
1 tablespoon butter
2 tomatoes, seeded and chopped
¾ cup seasoned bread crumbs
3 eggs, lightly beaten
salt and pepper to taste
1 whole mackerel (about 3 pounds)

Sauté the onions, mushrooms, and garlic in the oil and butter. Mix with the tomatoes, bread crumbs, and lightly beaten eggs. Add salt and pepper. Stuff the mackerel with this mixture. Sew it up or tie securely. Bake in a preheated 450° oven for about 20 minutes or until the fish flakes easily. Serve with Mustard Sauce or a tomato sauce or mayonnaise.

Serves 4 to 6.

Mustard Sauce

4 tablespoons butter
3 tablespoons flour
½ cup fish stock or bottled clam juice
1 cup milk
salt, pepper, and nutmeg, to taste
1 tablespoon Dijon mustard
1 teaspoon dry mustard

Melt the butter in a saucepan, add the flour, and whisk for 1 minute. Add the stock or clam juice and the milk and whisk until it has thickened. Add the seasonings and mustards, and serve over the fish.

Serves 4 to 6.

Crabmeat Florentine

Another fairly quick recipe that is both easy enough for family and fancy enough for company. Crabmeat is a staple in the local markets, so we tend to forget what a delicacy it really is.

2 packages frozen spinach
3 tablespoons butter
2 tablespoons shallots, minced
3 tablespoons flour
1⅔ cups milk
⅓ cup half-and-half
pinch of cayenne pepper
pinch of nutmeg
½ teaspoon mustard powder
1 egg yolk, lightly beaten
2 tablespoons Swiss cheese, grated
1 pound fresh crabmeat
1 tablespoon Parmesan cheese, grated

Cook the spinach in a nonstick skillet until all the water has evaporated and it is barely tender. Place it in the bottom of a buttered gratin dish or shallow baking dish. Set aside.

In a 2-quart saucepan, melt the butter, and add the shallots and stir until softened. Add the flour, stirring with a wire whisk for 1 minute. In another pan or a microwave, combine the milk and cream and heat it to below a simmer. Whisk the warm milk mixture slowly into the butter and flour and stir until thickened. Add the cayenne, nutmeg, and mustard powder. Remove from the heat and add the lightly beaten egg yolk and the Swiss cheese. Stir until the cheese has melted. Arrange the crabmeat over the spinach, pour the sauce over all, and sprinkle with the Parmesan cheese. Bake in a preheated 350° oven for 10 to 15 minutes or until heated through.

Serves 6 to 8.

❊ ❊ ❊

Some Personal Experiences

Peter Cohen (Sally's husband)
Hancock natives referring to the people who live in Bar Harbor: "Theyah sittin' on theyah view."

Robert Rohe (Terry's husband)
Finishing up a conversation with a Port Clyde lobsterman: "Have a good day."
Lobsterman: "Don't tell me what to do!"

Terry Rohe
Terry: "Hey, shake, I'm seventy-five too."
Lobsterman: (After a swift appraising look)
"Well, you're steaming along pretty good."

Meat and Poultry

Although, as you might expect, a great deal of fish is eaten in Maine, meat and chicken entrées still vie for center stage. These recipes tend to be of the hearty variety, just the thing to warm one up after a long day on the lobster boat or cutting Christmas trees.

Many Mainers work at a variety of jobs. The mussel dragger helps out with the Christmas wreaths in November and December, and the folks who harvest the wild blueberries may also be the ones who plow the roads in January. And whatever they do, they love to eat!

New England Boiled Dinner

Our version of this classic recipe. Serve with a bowl of horseradish.

5 to 6 pounds corned beef
½ pound salt pork
1 cabbage, quartered
3 small white turnips or 1 yellow turnip, quartered
4 to 6 carrots, scraped
4 small parsnips, peeled and cut in ¼-inch rounds
6 potatoes, skins on, sliced
6 beets
salt and pepper to taste
butter to taste (for beets)

The corned beef may be brisket, rump, or thick rib. Soak the beef in water for 1 hour or more. Drain, then cook in fresh water until tender (4 to 5 hours). After the first hour, add the salt pork. During the last hour, add all the vegetables except the beets. Boil the beets separately.

To serve, place the beef and pork in the center of a large platter and surround the meat with all the vegetables and potatoes except the beets. To eliminate the meal's turning beet red, serve them separately with the butter, salt, and pepper. Save all the leftovers for Red Flannel Hash.

Serves 6.

Red Flannel Hash

The secret lies in the beets. You can, and should, throw in any other leftover vegetables from your Boiled Dinner (recipe preceding), but the beets are the one "must have."

4 tablespoons beef suet cut in ¼-inch cubes
1 large onion, chopped fine
1 cup stock from Boiled Dinner, reduced to ½ cup
3 to 4 cups diced, cooked potatoes
2 cups leftover corned beef
1½ cups cooked diced beets
1½ cups leftover vegetables from New England Boiled
      Dinner (carrots, turnips, cabbage, etc.)
1 teaspoon Worcestershire sauce

In a large cast-iron frying pan, try out the suet, then skim out the cubes. Drain most of the fat, add the onion, and sauté until soft. Add the rest of the ingredients, turn the heat very low, and smooth the mixture in the pan (but don't mash down). Cook it until it begins to brown around the edges, about 45 minutes.

    Have a large, round, warmed platter ready. Carefully loosen the hash around the edges. VERY carefully (steady, now) flip the pan over the platter as you would an omelet. Sprinkle suet cracklings over the top.

Serves 6.

Norwegian Potpourri

A Norwegian neighbor gave us this family recipe, which is a Scandinavian version of the Maine classic. If you can't find fresh dill, leave it out.

4 cups leftover cooked chicken, ham, beef, or lamb, or
    some of each
2 cooked leeks, cut in chunks
2 cups frozen peas
4 tomatoes, quartered
½ cup diced, cooked potatoes
1 tablespoon butter
2 tablespoons flour
2 cups beef bouillon
½ cup dry Madeira wine
1 teaspoon soy sauce
pepper to taste
1 tablespoon fresh chopped dill

Place the diced meats and the vegetables in a large casserole. Melt the butter in a saucepan and stir until it begins to brown. Add the flour and continue stirring for 1 minute over low heat. Add the bouillon and cook for 3 to 4 minutes more, stirring constantly. Stir in the Madeira, soy sauce, pepper, and dill. Pour the sauce over the ingredients, cover the casserole, and heat thoroughly in 375° oven.

Serves 6 to 8.

Oven-Barbecued Brisket

One of the major charms of this recipe is that everything is cooked together in a foil package and unwrapped at the moment of truth, just before serving. If you're careful, there's absolutely no cleanup. The brisket may be served with rice, or you can cube some potatoes and put them in the package, too.

4 to 5 pounds lean beef brisket
¾ cup tomato puree
1 teaspoon Worcestershire sauce
1 teaspoon vinegar
1 tablespoon brown sugar
2 tablespoons vegetable oil
½ teaspoon thyme
½ teaspoon dry mustard
salt and pepper to taste
2 or 3 dashes cayenne pepper
3 medium carrots, sliced lengthwise

Preheat oven to 350°. Place the brisket on a piece of heavy (or double) aluminum foil, large enough to completely package the beef and vegetables for baking. Combine the remaining ingredients except the carrots in a saucepan and bring to a boil. Place the carrots on top of the meat and pour the sauce over all. Seal the edges of foil as though it were an envelope, pinching them carefully. Place on a baking sheet and bake for 2½ to 3 hours or until the meat is fork tender.

Serves 6.

Lamb Stew

Because raising sheep, especially on the islands dotting the coast-line, has a long history in Maine, lamb is a favorite meat—and we think one of the most elegantly flavorful.

1 large onion, chopped
1 clove garlic, minced
2 tablespoons canola oil
1½ pounds lean lamb, cubed
1 cup crushed tomatoes
1 cup frozen tiny white onions
1 cup chicken broth
2 cups carrots, cut in 2-inch chunks
1½ cups peeled, diced potatoes
1 cup peeled white turnips, cut in ½-inch dice
¾ cup frozen peas
salt and pepper to taste

In a large, flame-proof casserole, sauté the onion and garlic in the oil until soft. Add the lamb and continue cooking until it has lost its raw color. Add the tomatoes, white onions, chicken broth, carrots, potatoes, and turnips. Cover and simmer on low heat until the lamb is tender, about 1 to 1½ hours. Add the peas and cook an additional 10 minutes. Add the salt and pepper. Serve hot, with French bread to mop up the wonderful gravy.

Serves 4 to 6.

Party Baked-Beef Stew

One of the greatest attributes of this stew is that it's so laid back. It cooks for 6 hours in a low, low oven and tastes even better the next day, so that if you're really stressed out you can make it the day before the party and reheat it.

3 pounds lean beef, cubed
3 large onions, thinly sliced
2 tablespoons canola oil
1 15-ounce can crushed tomatoes
10 large dried prunes
2 bay leaves
1 teaspoon chopped garlic
2 tablespoons paprika
2 tablespoons barley
salt and pepper to taste
¼ cup dry vermouth
2 cups water
4 tablespoons light sour cream

Brown the meat and onions in the oil in a large Dutch oven. Add the tomatoes, prunes, bay leaves, garlic, paprika, barley, salt and pepper, vermouth, and water. Cover and bake in a preheated 375° oven for 20 minutes. Turn the oven down to 200° and bake for 6 hours. If the stew seems dry, you may add a bit more water. Add the sour cream, stir, and serve over broad noodles or rice, or on its own with a salad and French bread.

Serves 6 to 8.

Chili

It's so easy to keep the ingredients for chili in the house (including frozen ground beef, which you then defrost in the microwave), and you can use cut-up veggies (zucchini, eggplant, cooked carrots, or whatever) for a vegetarian version. It's about 40 minutes from start to finish, kids as well as adults love it, and we use the leftovers for making stuffed green peppers.

2 tablespoons good-quality olive oil
2 medium onions, chopped
2 cloves garlic, chopped
1 pound ground chuck
2 15-ounce cans crushed tomatoes
5 tablespoons regular chili powder (or to taste)
2 tablespoons hot chili powder (or to taste)
1 teaspoon ground cumin
1 teaspoon dried oregano
½ teaspoon paprika
⅛ teaspoon cayenne pepper
1 tablespoon red wine vinegar
pinch sugar
2 cans pinto beans, drained and rinsed

Gather and measure all the ingredients. Heat the oil in a heavy, flameproof 5-quart pot. Sauté the onion and garlic until they are soft, then add the meat and brown. Add the tomatoes, chili powders, cumin, oregano, paprika, cayenne pepper, vinegar, and sugar. Cook, uncovered, for 20 minutes on low heat, stirring occasionally. Add the pinto beans and simmer another 10 minutes. This is a fairly "hot" chili. Add chili powders 1 tablespoon at a time until the taste is to your liking.

Serves 6.

Stuffed Green Peppers

We use left-over Chili for this dish. If you are fresh out of that, you can use homemade or bottled sauce (Paul Newman's is great) instead. These freeze well, too.

3 large green peppers
1 tablespoon olive oil
1 medium onion, finely diced
4 to 6 mushrooms, wiped and diced
¾ cup rice
¾ cup chicken stock
1 cup leftover Chili, spaghetti sauce, or tomato sauce
½ pound ground beef or turkey, cooked (optional)
½ cup grated Cheddar cheese

Parboil the green peppers in boiling water for 2 minutes. Halve and remove the seeds and membranes. Place open-side-up in a baking pan coated with the olive oil. In a 2-quart saucepan, sauté the onion and mushrooms until soft. Add the rice, chicken stock, and chili or sauce and cook, covered, on low heat for about 15 minutes or until the rice is nearly tender. Add the optional meat. Stuff the peppers with the rice mixture, sprinkle the grated cheese on top, and bake in a preheated 350° oven for 20 to 25 minutes.

Serves 6.

Down East Nuclear Meat Loaf

Another way to use up leftovers. This is so good, we've been known to use "store-bought" beans. A cold meat loaf sandwich with ketchup and red onion, a glass of cider, and a Patriots game is a first rate recipe for a Sunday afternoon.

1 medium onion, chopped
1 clove garlic, minced
1 pound ground beef
1 10-ounce can barbecue-baked beans, partially drained, or
    1 cup leftover home-baked beans
¼ cup seasoned bread crumbs
1 egg
¼ cup ketchup

Spray a baking pan with vegetable spray. Place all the ingredients in a large bowl, roll up your sleeves, and mix everything together with your hands. When it is thoroughly mixed, form into a loaf shape and place in the baking dish. Bake in a preheated 350° oven for 1 hour.

Serves 4 to 6.

Hamburger Noodle Casserole

We don't know what it is about this one, but all kids seem to love it. It dates back to the 1940s.

1/2 pound noodles or elbow macaroni
1 medium onion, finely diced
1/2 cup mushrooms, diced
1 tablespoon canola oil
1 pound lean ground beef
1 can condensed cream of tomato soup
1 cup sharp Cheddar cheese, grated

Boil the noodles until they are almost tender, drain, and set aside. In a skillet, sauté the onion and mushrooms in the oil until they are soft. Add the ground beef and brown. Drain any accumulated fat and place the meat mixture in a 2- or 3-quart casserole. Add the tomato soup, noodles, and cheese and stir well. Bake in a preheated 350° oven for 1/2 hour or until top is slightly crusty.

Serves 4.

Creamed Ham

A grand lunch or Sunday supper dish, it also works well with chicken. If using chicken, make white sauce with ¾ cup milk and ¾ cup undiluted uncondensed chicken broth.

4 tablespoons butter or margarine
3 tablespoons all-purpose flour
1½ cups milk
2 cups ham, cooked and diced
3 tablespoons pimento, finely chopped
2 tablespoons sherry
salt and pepper to taste
6 patty shells, baked, or toasted English muffin halves
2 tablespoons parsley, chopped

In a 2-quart saucepan, melt the butter, then add the flour, stirring constantly with a wire whisk. Add the milk slowly, continuing to whisk, until the sauce is thickened. Keep the sauce warm over hot water. Add the ham, pimento, sherry, salt, and pepper.

Meanwhile, prepare the patty shells according to the package directions. Place the shells or muffins on a serving platter or individual plates. Make sure the ham sauce is piping hot. Spoon the sauce into the shells or over the muffins and garnish with the chopped parsley.

Serves 6.

Ham-Potato Cakes

You won't believe what a wonderful flavor these little beauties have. Fresh green beans and a crisp coleslaw make admirable accompaniments.

3 cups minced ham
3 cups mashed potatoes
1 egg, beaten
1 teaspoon parsley, minced
½ teaspoon prepared mustard (or more, to taste)
salt, pepper, and paprika to taste
flour for dusting
2 to 3 tablespoons butter or margarine for frying

Beat together the ham, potatoes, and egg. Beat in the parsley and mustard and season to taste. Form into patties, dust with the flour, and fry in the butter or margarine until brown on both sides.

Serves 4.

Pineapple Upside-Down Ham Loaf

You might guess this to be a combination upside-down cake and ham loaf—and you'd be right!

3 tablespoons butter
⅓ cup light brown sugar
6 to 9 pineapple slices
6 to 9 maraschino cherries
1 pound ground, cooked ham
⅔ pound raw pork, freshly ground
2 cups plain bread crumbs
2 eggs, beaten
1 cup milk
salt and pepper to taste
½ teaspoon dry mustard

Melt the butter with the brown sugar and place in the bottom of an 8-by-8-by-2-inch square pan. Place a layer of pineapple slices on the sugar and drop a cherry into the center of each. Mix together the remaining ingredients and spread evenly on top of the fruit. Bake at 350° for 1½ hours. Turn out onto a serving platter and cut into squares.

Serves 6.

Glazed Ham Steak

A way to have all the flavor in a big, juicy baked ham for just four people.

2 tablespoons butter or margarine
1 tablespoon undiluted frozen orange juice
1/4 cup packed dark brown sugar
1/2 tablespoon prepared mustard
1 or 2 ham steaks about 1/2 inch thick, a total weight of
    about 1 1/4 to 1 1/2 pounds

Melt the butter in a large skillet and add the orange juice, brown sugar, and mustard. Mix well. Place the ham steaks in this mixture and cook over medium heat 3 to 4 minutes per side or until nicely browned. Serve with a green vegetable and baked sweet potatoes.

Serves 4.

Country Pork Chops

A casserole for mid-winter when there's a foot of snow outside and you know everyone's going to be ravenous. Easily doubled for a dinner party, and you can get all but the final baking done ahead of time.

6 loin pork chops, 1 inch thick
½ cup celery, diced
½ cup carrots, diced
½ cup onions, diced
salt and pepper to taste
½ cup beef stock or bouillon
½ cup tomato sauce
2 tablespoons Dijon mustard
2 teaspoons Worcestershire sauce
½ cup parsley, chopped

Brown the chops on both sides in a large nonstick skillet for 8 minutes on each side. Arrange the mixed vegetables on the bottom of a shallow casserole. Place the chops on the bed of veggies. Salt and pepper to taste. Mix the stock, tomato sauce, mustard, and Worcestershire sauce and pour over the chops. Sprinkle with parsley. Cover and bake for 50 minutes; uncover and bake for 10 to 15 minutes more. Serve with rice pilaf or baked potatoes.

Serves 6.

Mom's Pork Roast and Sauerkraut

This recipe comes from Sally's mother, who got it from her mother. It is definitely "from away" but has been adopted enthusiastically by local friends. It's good enough to serve to company and often is.

2 to 2½ pounds pork tenderloin
2 pounds sauerkraut
3 or 4 large apples, peeled, cored, and sliced
¾ cup (or to taste) dark brown sugar, packed
1 large can Italian-style tomato chunks
1 medium onion, sliced thin

Place the pork in a large oven-proof casserole, kettle, or baking pan. Drain and rinse the sauerkraut, saving the juice. Spread ½ of the sauerkraut around the pork. Place a layer of apple slices on top of the sauerkraut. Sprinkle ½ of the brown sugar over the apples. Squish the tomatoes in your fingers and spread ½ of them over the apples. Layer ½ of the onions over the tomatoes.

Repeat with the rest of the sauerkraut, apples, sugar, onions, and tomatoes, ending with the tomatoes. Pour the juices from the tomatoes and the sauerkraut around the roast. Bake in a preheated 350° oven for 1 hour and 15 minutes or until a meat thermometer registers 155°. This is wonderful served with mashed potatoes and cinnamon apple sauce.

Serves 6 to 8.

Easy Baked Chicken

And when we say easy, we mean it. Three ingredients, including the chicken. Adding the mustard sauce turns it into company fare.

4 chicken breast halves, boned and skinned
2 tablespoons mayonnaise
½ to ⅓ cup Italian seasoned bread crumbs

Coat each chicken piece with the mayonnaise. Dip breasts (both sides) in the bread crumbs. Bake in a preheated 350° oven for 20 to 25 minutes.

Serves 4.

Mustard Sauce

¾ cup light mayonnaise
2 teaspoons of an interesting mustard of your choice

Mix the mayonnaise and the mustard. Heat for 8 to 10 seconds in a microwave. Watch it if your microwave is powerful; it doesn't take long. And there you have it!

Serves 4.

Chicken Quiche

*Some people think making a quiche is a tricky proposition. Well,
it's not. A quiche is essentially a custard pie to which you add
anything in the world from chicken to veggies to seafood. It's a
great lunch dish; and if you bake it in a square dish, you can cut
it into small pieces for starters.*

1 whole skinless chicken breast, poached and cubed (reserve
    liquid for future use)
1 onion, halved, and bunch of celery tops for poaching liquid
2 tablespoons shallots or green onions, minced
½ pound fresh mushrooms, wiped and sliced
3 tablespoons butter
1 teaspoon lemon juice
3 eggs
½ cup whipping cream
½ teaspoon dried tarragon
¼ teaspoon salt
1 partially baked 9-inch pie crust
¼ cup grated Swiss cheese
1 tablespoon butter, cut into pea-size dots

Poach the chicken in water or stock to cover, adding the
onion and celery before cooking. Cook the shallots or green
onions and mushrooms in the butter in a heavy-bottomed
saucepan until soft. Add the lemon juice, stir in the
chicken, and set aside.
    Lightly beat the eggs, cream, and tarragon. Add the
chicken, mushroom mixture, and salt, and pour into a
partially baked pie crust. Sprinkle with the grated cheese,
dot with the cut-up butter, and bake at 375° for 25 to
30 minutes.

Serves 6.

Chicken Pot Pie

There used to be lots of chicken farmers in Maine, but no more. Chicken dishes, however, still rank near the top of any local hit parade. This is one that's been around for generations, and when you try it, you'll understand why.

4 slices bacon
1½ large onions, chopped fine
½ cup sliced fresh mushrooms
2 tablespoons butter
2 tablespoons flour
2 cups chicken, cooked and diced, broth reserved
1 cup cream
2 egg yolks, slightly beaten
1 cup peas, fresh or frozen
4 medium potatoes, cooked and diced
1 prepared pastry crust

Cook the bacon until just crisp. Remove with a slotted spoon, drain, and place on the bottom of a 2½-quart casserole. Sauté the onions and mushrooms in the bacon fat until just tender. Set aside.

Make a roux by melting the 2 tablespoons of butter in a saucepan and adding the 2 tablespoons of flour, mixing with a whisk. Add the reserved chicken broth, 1 cup cream, and 2 egg yolks, whisking all the time. Add the 2 cups cooked chicken to the sauce. Mix in the mushrooms, onions, peas, and potatoes into the sauce, then pour everything into the casserole over the bacon. Cover with the prepared pastry crust, pricking the crust with a fork in several places. Place in a preheated 350° oven for 50 to 60 minutes, until the crust is brown.

Alternate method: bake without the crust for 45 minutes, then cover the ingredients with biscuit rounds, turn the oven up to 450°, and bake 15 minutes longer.

Serves 6.

Sautéed Chicken Breasts with Raspberry Vinegar

What a felicitous marriage of flavors! The whole process takes about 10 minutes and the resulting dish is complex and full of character. Just as good cold as hot. Great for a boat picnic!

2 whole chicken breasts (4 halves), about 1½ pounds total
salt and ground white pepper to taste
2 teaspoons or more dried tarragon
2 tablespoons butter
2 tablespoons canola oil
1 tablespoon shallots, finely minced
¼ cup raspberry vinegar
¼ cup chicken broth

Cut the breasts so that you have 4 halves. Lightly salt and pepper them. Sprinkle them on both sides with the tarragon.

Place 1 tablespoon each of the butter and oil in a heavy skillet. Sauté the shallots until they are soft and beginning to brown. Add the chicken breasts and cook over medium heat until browned on both sides. Add ½ of the vinegar and chicken broth and continue cooking for 5 minutes. Turn the breasts, add the rest of the vinegar and broth, and cook for 2 to 3 minutes more.

Remove the breasts to a serving platter. Reduce the liquid until it thickens slightly, pour it over the breasts, and serve.

Serves 4.

Baked Chicken Hash

*This casserole is a big multi-generational favorite. We love it
with canned cinnamon apple rounds or Betty Mae's Plum
Chutney (page 153).*

2 tablespoons butter
1½ tablespoons flour
1 cup chicken stock
salt and white ground pepper to taste
¼ teaspoon rosemary
2 cups cooked chicken, diced
1 cup cooked carrots and peas
½ cup bread crumbs

Make a white sauce by heating together the butter and flour
and thickening with the chicken stock instead of the cus-
tomary milk. Add the seasonings and cook over *very* low
heat (or in a double boiler). Stir in the chicken and the carrots and peas. Turn the mixture into a buttered casserole.
Sprinkle with the bread crumbs and bake in a preheated
350° oven for 30 minutes or until the top has browned.

Serves 4 to 6.

Chicken Dorothe

Dorothe never used measurements for this recipe; she just kept sprinkling and pouring until it looked and smelled right. We tend to make it the same way. We have tried to give some idea of the amounts of things, but if you have a hankering to dismiss all that, just sprinkle and pour until it looks and smells right.

1 large onion or more, sliced thin
2 to 3 pounds chicken parts
1 tablespoon garlic powder (one of the very few recipes in
    which we use it)
salt and freshly ground pepper
1 tablespoon paprika
¼ cup ketchup
1 cup unsalted chicken broth
½ package onion soup mix (Lipton's preferred)

In a rectangular 8-by-14-inch baking dish, spread out all the onion rings on the bottom of the pan. Sprinkle each piece of chicken, front and back, with garlic powder, salt, pepper, and paprika. Lay the chicken pieces, skin side up, on the bed of onions. Mix together the ketchup, chicken broth, and onion soup mix, and pour it carefully around the chicken, trying not to wash the seasonings off.

Place the chicken in a preheated 300° oven. After the first 10 to 15 minutes the seasonings will have bonded to the chicken; therefore, you may now baste the chicken with the liquid in the pan. After another 15 minutes or so of basting and baking, cover the chicken with aluminum foil and cook undisturbed for an additional hour and 15 minutes. Finally, remove the foil and cook uncovered, basting once or twice more, for 10 minutes. Total cooking time is around 2 hours.

Serves 4 to 6 hearty eaters.

Turkey Cutlets Marsala

This dish is usually made with veal, an expensive—though elegant—cut of meat. Our version uses turkey cutlets, and while you're counting your change, you can also congratulate yourself on how little fat there is in this recipe.

1¼ pounds turkey cutlets
salt and pepper to taste
flour for dredging
2 tablespoons butter
1 cup mushrooms, wiped and sliced
¼ cup chicken stock
⅓ cup Marsala
¼ cup chopped parsley

Flatten the cutlets with the flat side of a meat hammer. Add the salt and pepper to the flour. Place it in a paper sack and, one by one, lightly dredge the cutlets by shaking them inside the bag until they are evenly coated.

Melt the butter in a nonstick skillet and sauté the mushrooms until they are tender and golden brown. Reserve the mushrooms. Add a couple of tablespoons of the stock to the skillet, and when it is hot, place the turkey cutlets in and sauté over medium-high heat until browned, about 45 seconds to 1 minute on each side. Add 1 or 2 tablespoons of remaining stock if cutlets become too dry.

Remove the turkey to a platter and keep warm. Add the Marsala to the skillet and simmer it for 2 to 3 minutes until it is slightly reduced. Add the cooked mushrooms to the sauce and pour it over the turkey. Sprinkle with the parsley and serve immediately.

Serves 4.

Country Pot Roast

1 3- to 4-pound beef brisket or bottom round roast
1 tablespoon paprika (approximately)
pepper to taste
1 tablespoon garlic powder
½ teaspoon minced garlic
1 tablespoon canola oil
1 package onion soup mix
1 cup water
¼ cup ketchup
1 onion, sliced
4 russet potatoes, peeled and cut in quarters
4 carrots, cut in chunks

Sprinkle the meat with the paprika, pepper, and garlic
powder. In a large Dutch oven, sear the meat in the oil
over high heat until browned on all sides. Remove from the
heat. Mix the packaged onion soup mix, the water, the
garlic, and the ketchup. Place the onion, potatoes, and
carrots around the roast in the Dutch oven. Pour the water
and onion soup mixture over the meat.

Place the top on the pot and place the pot in a preheated 325° oven. Bake for 2 to 2¼ hours or until the meat
is fork tender. Take the meat out of the pot and let it cool
for a few minutes, then slice and place on a warm platter.
Surround with the potatoes, carrots, and onions. Drizzle
some of the juice over the meat and serve the rest of the
pan juices on the side.

Serves 6.

Salads, Dressings, Sauces, and Preserves

Sometimes a salad is a bit of butter lettuce on a plate with half an avocado resting in its folds. Sometimes it's a hearty meal containing meat and vegetables, or pasta. Sometimes it's hot, other times cold. There really are no rules to break. The same is true for sauces. They go on entrées, on desserts, or just on your plate next to a cookie. Here's a Maine selection.

WHOLE MEAL SALADS

Curried Chicken Salad

In Sally's catering business this is the favorite salad for a luncheon, buffet supper, or picnic. When we serve it to a large number of people, we often make it into easy-to-manage sandwiches by halving small whole-wheat pita breads and stuffing them with the chicken mixture and then piling dill sprouts on top. If served on plates, juicy seedless green grapes are a nice addition.

4 cups cooked chicken breasts, skinned and cut into chunks
5 cored Granny Smith apples, cubed, skins left on
5 stalks celery, diced fine
5 scallions, finely chopped, whites and half of greens
1 cup mayonnaise
1 cup light sour cream
1½ tablespoons curry powder, or to taste
salt to taste
1 cup chopped walnuts
½ pound seedless green grapes (optional)

Place the first 4 ingredients in a large bowl. In another bowl, mix the mayonnaise, sour cream, curry powder, and salt together. Add the mayonnaise mixture to the chicken. Add the nuts and the grapes, if used. Mound on a lettuce-lined serving platter and garnish with branches of grapes.

Serves 8 to 10.

Best Potato Salad

4 large red or russet potatoes (2 to 3 pounds), unpeeled,
    cooked, and diced
1 large red onion, finely diced
3 or 4 stalks celery, finely diced
1/4 cup green olives, chopped
1 small green pepper, seeded and diced (optional)
1/2 to 3/4 cup mayonnaise
1 tablespoon Dijon mustard
salt and freshly ground black pepper to taste

Mix all of the ingredients in a large bowl. Taste and correct
the seasonings. Keep refrigerated until ready to serve.

Serves 6.

Lobster and Wild Rice Salad

A nice, if extravagant, way to usher in the summer.

3 cups cooked wild rice
2 cups cooked lobster
2 or 3 scallions, top third discarded, cut in 2-inch
 julienne strips
1 cup cooked cold asparagus, cut in 2-inch sections
½ cup slivered almonds
½ cup watercress, coarsely diced
½ to 1 cup Mustard Vinaigrette (page 146)
salt and pepper to taste

Combine all the ingredients in a large bowl, adding only
½ cup of the Mustard Vinaigrette to start. Toss gently until
the dressing is thoroughly mixed. Refrigerate for 2 hours.
Before serving, taste the salad and add more dressing if
needed. Garnish with more watercress and serve on a large
platter or on individual plates.

Serves 6.

Crab-Stuffed Tomato Cups

Our growing season is short so we try to make the most out of every last gorgeous, juicy tomato that appears on our horizon. Our crabmeat is plentiful and superb. We hope you'll agree that the following union is a marriage made in heaven.

4 large, ripe tomatoes
8 ounces crabmeat
2 tablespoons green onions, minced
½ cup celery, finely diced
1 teaspoon Dijon mustard
fresh lemon juice to taste
salt and pepper to taste
1 cup mayonnaise

Wash the tomatoes and cut 1 slice off the top. Seed the tomatoes by scooping them out with a spoon, saving as much of the flesh as you can but allowing room for a good scoop of salad in each.

Toss the flaked crabmeat, onions, and celery together. Add the mustard, lemon juice, salt, and pepper to the mayonnaise. Mix the crabmeat with the mayonnaise. Fill each tomato with as much crab mixture as it will hold, mounding it up. Serve on a bed of lettuce.

Serves 4.

VEGETABLE SALADS

Tomato Aspic

*We aren't sure just what it is about this jellied vegetable salad,
but people always ask for the recipe. It has deep and intense
flavor, wonderful crunch and texture. If you don't want to serve
it in a ring mold, you can make little individual molds.*

3 envelopes gelatin
2 cups cold V-8 juice
2½ cups hot beef bouillon
1½ teaspoons Worcestershire sauce
4 to 6 drops Tabasco sauce
6 tablespoons lemon juice
1 cup celery, finely diced
½ cup cucumber, finely diced
1/2 cup radishes, finely diced
other chopped raw vegetables of your choice such as
        carrots, green peppers (optional)
1 tablespoon chopped fresh dill weed or 1 teaspoon dried
1 or 2 diced scallions

In a large bowl, sprinkle the gelatin over the cold juice and
let it stand for 1 or 2 minutes. Add the hot bouillon and stir
until the gelatin is completely dissolved. Stir in the other
ingredients. Oil the inside of a 5½- or 6-quart ring mold
and pour the aspic into the mold. Chill for 5 or 6 hours or,
even better, overnight.

Unmold by dipping the container in a bowl of very
warm water for a brief few seconds. Place a serving plate on
top of the mold, turn both over together, and shake. If you
are lucky, the salad will drop out. If not, try loosening
edges with a knife and try the whole thing again.

Serves 10.

Four Bean Salad

Generally we prefer fresh over canned every time. There are exceptions to every rule, and this is one of them. To those of you who feel it would be better using fresh beans, be our guest; we know it tastes wonderful that way, too. Our excuse is that this is the way it tasted when our grandmothers made it.

1 can green beans
1 can yellow waxed beans
1 can garbanzo beans
1 can red kidney beans
1 green pepper, thinly sliced
1 red Bermuda onion, thinly sliced
Mustard Vinaigrette (page 146)

Drain all the beans and empty into a large salad bowl. Glass is especially nice as it lets you enjoy all the beautiful colors in this salad. Mix in the green pepper and Bermuda onion, and dress with enough Mustard Vinaigrette to coat all the ingredients without ending up with a pool of dressing at the bottom of the bowl. Chill and serve.

Serves 4 to 6.

Cucumber Salad

This is the best stuff! It's crunchy. It's sweet. It's sour. You'll love it. Trust us.

2 large cucumbers, peeled and thinly sliced
salt, perhaps 1 tablespoon
1 cup white vinegar
½ cup sugar
⅛ teaspoon freshly ground black pepper
2 tablespoons chopped fresh dill

Sprinkle the cucumbers lightly with salt and let them stand for about 1 hour. Rinse well, drain, and press the water out of them with paper towels. Place in a glass or china serving dish. Combine the vinegar, sugar, pepper, and dill and let stand for a few minutes. Pour over the cucumbers and chill for 2 or 3 hours or as long as overnight.

Serves 6.

Waldorf Salad

Who knows if it's true or not, but this salad was supposed to have originated at the Waldorf–Astoria Hotel in New York City. Most Mainers know only that it's a salad most of them grew up with. Since we became aware of the splendor and abundance of their hardy apple crop, we haven't wondered that it's a state favorite.

6 large tart apples (Granny Smith or Cortland or both)
3 cups finely chopped celery
1 cup, more or less, best-quality mayonnaise
1 cup chopped walnuts

Wash and core the apples, but do not peel. Cut them into small cubes. Add the chopped celery and the mayonnaise, starting with ½ cup and adding by the spoonful until all the fruit is coated. Add the walnuts and mix well, adding a bit more mayonnaise if necessary. Mound the salad on a pretty platter upon a layer of romaine lettuce. Arrange small bunches of seedless green grapes around the edges of the salad and refrigerate until ready to serve.

Serves 6 to 8.

Spinach, Orange, and Mushroom Salad with Orange Vinaigrette

3 navel oranges, peeled
1 teaspoon grated fresh orange zest
2 tablespoons fresh orange juice
2 tablespoons fresh lemon juice
1 teaspoon Dijon mustard
⅔ cup walnut oil
salt to taste
2 pounds fresh spinach, carefully washed and dried
½ pound fresh mushrooms, wiped and sliced
½ cup coarsely chopped walnuts

Section the peeled oranges, halve crosswise, and set aside. In a small, high-sided bowl, mix the orange zest, orange juice, lemon juice, and mustard with a small wire whisk. Pour the walnut oil into the orange-mustard mixture in a slow stream, whisking hard until all the oil has been added and the dressing has emulsified. Add salt to taste.

Place the spinach in a large bowl and add the reserved oranges, the mushrooms, and the walnuts. Add ½ the dressing, taste, and continue to add dressing until all the leaves are coated but not so much that there is liquid at the bottom of the bowl. The remainder of the dressing will keep for up to a week if stored in a tightly closed bottle.

Serves 6 to 8.

DRESSINGS, SAUCES, AND PRESERVES

Herbed Mayonnaise

We sometimes make our own mayonnaise but more often use a good quality prepared one since the safety of fresh eggs is now known to be iffy. Here is a recipe for herbed mayonnaise that will keep, tightly covered and refrigerated, for several days and that can be used on seafood salads, potato salad, and as the base for hot sauces that are great with meat and chicken.

1 cup good-quality real mayonnaise, bottled
any or all of the following: basil, oregano, marjoram, thyme,
    rosemary, dill, tarragon

Fresh crushed garlic or mustard may also be added, but their flavors are so strong that they should usually be used alone, with each other, or with just one other flavor. Mix the ingredients and refrigerate the unused portion in a tightly closed bottle.

Makes 1 cup.

�֎ ✷ ✷

As recently as 1970 it was impossible to find garlic in grocery stores in Down East Maine. Terry, a journalist during the week in New York and a weekend cook at her country inn, arrived in Bangor each Friday night, wearing a garland of garlic for her Inn kitchen.

Mustard Vinaigrette

*Our basic salad dressing, and one of the best of its kind. It has a
secret ingredient.*

¾ cup best-quality virgin olive oil
1 or 2 garlic cloves, pressed in garlic press
1½ tablespoons brandy
2 tablespoons Dijon mustard
¼ cup, or a bit less, white wine vinegar
salt and freshly ground black pepper to taste

In a small, high-sided bowl, mix the olive oil, garlic,
brandy, and mustard. Let stand for 10 minutes. Add the
vinegar a little at a time, whisking hard with a small wire
whisk to emulsify the oil. Taste before you have added all
the vinegar and suit yourself. Add the salt and pepper.

Makes about 1 cup.

Dill Sauce for Fish

This is an adaptation of a sauce taught us by a Norwegian friend. You can double the recipe and keep it in the refrigerator for a week or longer. Everyone will want the recipe.

4 tablespoons old-fashioned rough-style mustard with seeds
1 teaspoon mustard powder
½ teaspoon lemon zest, freshly grated
2 tablespoons white wine vinegar
⅓ cup canola oil
4 tablespoons fresh dill, finely minced

In a small bowl with high sides, make a paste of the first four ingredients. Whisk in the oil as you would for mayonnaise, very slowly, whisking steadily until the sauce is very thick. Stir in the dill.

Makes about ¾ cup, enough to sauce fish for 4 to 6 persons.

Easy Sauce for Fish or Chicken

This sauce appears in various forms in several places in the cookbook. It's an easy solution and was taught us by a local innkeeper. His version was minus the sour cream, but we love the flavor when you put it in. It's wonderful either way.

1 cup good-quality mayonnaise
½ cup light sour cream
1½ tablespoons Dijon mustard
½ teaspoon dried tarragon (optional, but good if you're
    using the sauce for chicken)

Mix the ingredients together in a microwave-safe container. Microwave on low for about 15 to 20 seconds, just enough to heat through. Stir and serve over fish or chicken.

Makes 1½ cups.

Maine Blueberry Preserves with Curaçao

5 cups Maine wild blueberries, gently rinsed
3 cups sugar
1/4 cup curaçao or other orange liqueur

Mix the berries and sugar in a large pot. Heat gently until
the sugar melts. Add the curaçao and boil gently for 20 to
30 minutes, until a drop put on a clean, dry saucer tends to
stay put when the saucer is slightly tilted. If it runs very
easily it isn't done. Another test is to pour some slightly
cooled jam off a large, horizontally held spoon. If the jam
makes two drops instead of one along the lower edge of the
spoon, an inch or so apart, it's ready. Be patient. Pour the
hot preserves into hot, sterilized 8-ounce jars with discs and
rings.

You'll get a larger yield if you use pectin, following the
directions on the box, but somehow we prefer it the old-
fashioned way. I guess we're purists in the jam department.
This is so good over ice cream!

Makes 3 to 4 cups.

Marinade for Venison Roast

It used to be that you had to be or know a hunter to enjoy venison. In some places, deer are now being bred and raised for meat. Low in fat, high in flavor, venison needs long, slow cooking and is worth every minute of it.

1 carrot, sliced
3 onions, peeled and sliced
2 celery stalks, sliced
¼ cup olive oil
3 cups red wine
½ cup raspberry vinegar
fresh herbs, your choice, thyme, rosemary, and/or sage
12 peppercorns
12 juniper berries
¾ cup currants, plumped up in 1 cup hot red wine
½ teaspoon ground cloves
½ teaspoon ground cinnamon
2 teaspoons freshly grated ginger
2 tablespoons light brown sugar
½ cup heavy cream

Sauté the carrot, onion, and celery in the oil in a large Dutch oven or other heavy pot for about 10 minutes, or until they are soft. Add all of the other ingredients except the cream and simmer for 20 minutes. Cool and pour the marinade into a large glass bowl. Place a 3- to 4-pound venison roast in the bowl with the marinade, cover, and refrigerate for 1 to 3 days, turning several times.

To cook the roast, strain the marinade, reserving the onions, which should be placed back around the meat. Heat the strained marinade, pour over the meat, and bake in a preheated 375° oven for 2 hours or more until the meat is very tender. Remove roast and keep warm. Add the cream to the marinade and stir until combined. Slice the roast and serve with the creamy marinade.

Serves 6.

Blueberry Chutney

Usually when you think of chutney you think of apples or mangoes. Well, think again. Blueberries make a most unusual and savory chutney. We think you will enjoy this.

1 pound seedless raisins, diced
3 medium onions, peeled and chopped
2¼ pounds sugar
3 cups vinegar
2 tablespoons salt
2 tablespoons allspice
1 teaspoon pepper
2 tablespoons ground ginger
8 cups Maine wild blueberries, gently rinsed
2 cups apples, finely chopped

Put the raisins and onions through a food chopper. Bring the sugar, vinegar, and seasonings to a boil. Add the raisins, onions, blueberries, and apples to the vinegar mixture. Simmer this mixture all day and all night, if possible, or until the mixture becomes very black and very thick. Put into sterilized jars and seal with sterilized discs and rings.

Makes 4 pints.

Betty Mae's Plum Chutney

Betty Mae Rodwin is one of Sally's best and oldest friends and her former partner in "Crewel and Unusual," their stitchery manufacturing company. Although it is not, strictly, a Maine recipe, it goes well with so many Maine dishes that we have included it here.

This is a chutney for people who don't like chutney. We've never failed to make a convert with this one. It's a great mate for chicken, turkey, game, and curries of all kinds. This also makes a super Christmas gift, and it's very easy to double the recipe or halve it.

8 pounds fresh black (prune) plums
2 pounds brown sugar
2 pounds white sugar
2 cups cider vinegar
1 tablespoon ground cloves
1 tablespoon cinnamon
1 tablespoon allspice

While you are pitting the plums, bring the rest of the ingredients to a boil in a large pot. Add the plums and simmer gently for 2 to 3 hours. Put into sterilized jars and seal with sterilized discs and rings.

Makes approximately 10 pints.

Raspberry Sauce

Either do this in August when the raspberries are at their very best, or use the whole frozen berries, not in syrup. This sauce comes as close to heaven as products of the kitchen are likely to get.

2 quarts raspberries
1 quart sugar
¾ cup cold water

Mash the fruit, sprinkle with the sugar, and let stand overnight. Add the cold water and bring slowly to the boiling point. Cook 20 minutes. Force the berries through a double thickness of cheesecloth. Again, bring the sauce to the boiling point. Fill hot, sterilized jars and seal with sterilized discs and rings.

Makes 4 to 5 cups.

❈ ❈ ❈

Raspberries and blackberries were considered a nuisance, or at best used for medicinal purposes. In an early cookbook, blackberry syrup was recommended for cholera and "summer complaint." Mainers who worked as maids or gardeners for "summer people," frequently, and behind their backs, called **them** *"summer complaint."*

Hot Fudge Sauce

Beware! When you see how versatile and easy this is, you run the risk of chocoholism!

1 cup Nestlé chocolate chips OR 8 ounces Baker's
    German sweet chocolate OR 8 ounces Hershey's bar
    with nuts
⅛ to ¼ cup strong coffee, orange liqueur, amaretto, or
    whatever you like best

Place the chocolate and the liquid of your choice in a
microwave-safe serving bowl. Start with the smaller
amount; it's easier to add than to remove, although you can
always add a bit more chocolate. Heat in your microwave
for 10 seconds. Allow to sit for a couple of minutes. Remove from the microwave and stir until smooth. Add a bit
of water if it is too thick. If it is not entirely melted, microwave for another 4 or 5 seconds and stir again. You'll get it
right eventually. Results are sheer bliss!

Serves 6 to 8.

Apple Butter

People who are watching the amount of fat in their diet love this because they are truly satisfied by this aromatic, velvety, full-flavored spread on their morning toast. Those who don't care about fat are often converts anyway—it's that good.

12 large apples, stems removed (Cortland and Granny
      Smith are good choices)
1½ cups apple cider

Wash and cut the apples into quarters. Place in a large pot with the cider and boil until very soft. Put the apples through a food mill, and return the pulp to the pot. For each cup of pulp, add:

½ cup sugar
2 teaspoons cinnamon
1 teaspoon cloves
½ teaspoon allspice

Mix the sugar and spices with the apple pulp and boil gently, watching to see that it doesn't burn, for 8 to 10 minutes or until it's as thick as you like it. Pour into sterilized jars and cap with sterilized discs and rings.

Makes about 4 to 5 cups.

Strawberry Rhubarb Sauce

This wonderful combination can be used as a side dish or as a piquant dessert. As a filling for pie, it can seldom be equaled. There's something about the combination of flavors that's perfect.

4 cups rhubarb stalks cut into 2-inch pieces
1 to 2 cups sugar
1 pint fresh strawberries, hulled

Put the rhubarb pieces in a large saucepan and add 1 cup of the sugar. Let stand 3 or 4 hours or even overnight. Add the strawberries and bring the fruit to a boil. Simmer over low heat until the fruit is very tender. Taste to check on sweetness, being very careful not to burn your mouth. Add sugar, a little at a time, if you like a sweeter sauce; but the tartness is one of its pleasures, we think. Serve cold.

Serves 6 to 8.

※ ※ ※ ※ ※ ※ ※ ※ ※ ※ ※ ※ ※ ※

Vegetables

When we first moved to Down East Maine, we wondered why folks here bothered with gardens at all. The growing season is three months long at best. Home vegetable gardens are possible but take a lot more time, energy, and attention than Terry's long-ago patch in New Orleans, where the growing season is twice as long. We fight black flies, June freezes, gale-force summer winds, and rocky soil. And because of this enormous effort, the results of our struggle to foil Mother Nature are treasured beyond measure.

Green tomatoes get a lot of play because, around Labor Day, you know it could all be over any minute. Only for the past ten or fifteen years have imported fresh vegetables reached our markets all year long. What luxury!

Baked Apple and Carrot Casserole

One of the things that has always fascinated us is the interesting ways in which Mainers combine foods and flavors. This admirable side dish is great with poultry and game yet is sweet enough to serve as a dessert.

6 apples, cored, peeled, and thinly sliced
2 cups cooked carrot slices
$\frac{1}{3}$ cup brown sugar
2 tablespoons flour
salt to taste
$\frac{3}{4}$ cup orange juice

Place $\frac{1}{2}$ of the apples in a greased 2-quart baking dish and cover with $\frac{1}{2}$ of the carrots. Mix the brown sugar, flour, and salt and sprinkle $\frac{1}{2}$ of the mixture over the carrots. Repeat the layers and pour the orange juice over the top. Bake at 350° for 45 minutes.

Serves 6.

Ratatouille

This Mediterranean classic makes fine use of the things that grow in a Maine summer garden. The growing season is very short, and this recipe freezes well; therefore, when things are plentiful and at their peak, we make lots and freeze it in pint and quart containers. By the way, this is great over pasta.

½ cup olive oil
3 cloves garlic, minced
1 large onion, sliced
2 zucchini, scrubbed
1 small eggplant
3 tablespoons flour
2 green peppers, seeded and cut into strips
5 ripe tomatoes, sliced
¼ cup fresh dill, chopped
2 tablespoons dried basil
2 tablespoons dried oregano
salt and pepper

Heat the oil in a large skillet. Add the garlic and onion and sauté until transparent. Slice the zucchini, peel and cube the eggplant, and flour the pieces lightly. Add the zucchini, eggplant, and green peppers to the skillet. Cook, covered, over low heat for 1 hour or until soft, even mushy. Add the tomatoes, dill, basil, and oregano and simmer, uncovered, until mixture is thick. Season with the salt and pepper. Serve hot or cold.

Serves 4 as a vegetable, 8 as an appetizer.

Maine Vegetable Harvest Hash

This is the Down East version of ratatouille, and just as good!

1 ½ quarts salted water
2 large potatoes, quartered
1 head cabbage, core removed, quartered
1 medium onion, quartered
5 carrots, sliced lengthwise in quarters
2 stems fresh parsley, minced
2 tablespoons butter
2 tablespoons olive oil
½ cup bread crumbs, plain or seasoned
¼ cup grated Parmesan cheese
salt and pepper to taste

Put all the vegetables in the water along with the parsley and bring to a boil. Cook until they are *just* soft but not mushy. Strain the vegetables, reserve, and freeze the stock for a future soup. In a saucepan, melt the butter and olive oil. Gradually add the bread crumbs and cook until they are golden brown. In a large pot, combine this paste with the drained veggies and mash well until the mixture reaches the consistency of mashed potatoes. Add the Parmesan cheese, salt, and pepper and mix well. The vegetables can be put in a buttered casserole and reheated if they are not to be served immediately.

Serves 6.

FIDDLEHEAD FERNS

Maine's "signature" vegetable, this wild delicacy is tricky to harvest unless you know where to look. It's a little like hunting chanterelles, except that if you make a mistake it won't kill you. Now we are told that they are being shipped all over the country.

On each curled frond of the fern is a sort of brown scale or skin, which should be removed by wiping or by soaking in water and then wiping off. Also, there is a moment of truth with fiddleheads. They should be cooked and eaten no more than two days after picking. If you buy them in any part of the country other than New England, cook them the day you buy them. Use only the curled tip and from ½ to 2 inches of the stem.

Conventional wisdom states that the ferns taste like asparagus. The following 4 recipes will give a hint about the many things you can do with fiddlehead ferns.

Fiddleheads Au Naturel

1½ pounds of fiddleheads, washed and trimmed
3 quarts water, lightly salted
1 tablespoon butter
1 tablespoon fresh lemon juice
4 pieces toast (optional)

Plunge the fiddleheads into the boiling water and cook for 20 minutes. Drain and dress with the butter and lemon juice. Serve as a side dish or on toast.

Serves 4.

Fiddlehead Salad

1½ pounds fiddleheads, boiled and drained
1 cup thinly sliced red onion
3 tablespoons extra-virgin olive oil
1 tablespoon fresh lemon juice or raspberry vinegar
salt and pepper to taste

Boil the fiddleheads; drain and chill them. Place them in a bowl, add the rest of the ingredients, and return to the refrigerator, covered, for at least 2 hours.

Serves 4.

Fiddlehead Stir-Fry

1½ pounds fiddleheads, washed and trimmed
2 tablespoons olive oil
2 tablespoons sesame oil
1 tablespoon fresh ginger root, finely chopped
1 cup fresh snow peas, washed and trimmed
½ cup coarsely chopped cashews
1 tablespoon soy sauce

Remove the brown skin from each fiddlehead and trim to
½ to 2 inches below the curled tip. Pat dry in a paper
towel. Heat the oils together in a wok or large frying pan.
Add the ginger root and stir-fry for 1 minute. Add the fiddleheads and snow peas and stir-fry 4 to 5 minutes longer,
until tender but still crisp. Stir in the cashews and soy
sauce. Serve immediately over boiled rice.

Serves 6.

Fiddlehead MacMuffin

½ to ¾ pound fiddleheads
4 slices Canadian bacon, lightly browned in nonstick pan
4 halves English muffins, toasted
4 slices Cheddar cheese

Lightly steam the fiddleheads until soft but still firm (about 8 to 10 minutes). Place a slice of Canadian bacon on each muffin half. Drain the fiddleheads and place ¼ of them on top of each piece of Canadian bacon. Top each with a slice of the cheese. Place under the broiler until the cheese is melted.

Serves 4.

Scalloped Parsnips and Potatoes

This is another hearty mid-winter dish that certainly qualifies as comfort food. The wonderful locally grown potatoes make it all the better. If you're watching fat, use milk instead of cream.

4 good-sized parsnips, peeled and cut in rounds
4 large russet potatoes, peeled and cut in ¼-inch slices
2 to 3 tablespoons butter
salt and freshly ground pepper to taste
heavy cream to cover

Butter a 2-quart baking dish. Alternate layers of parsnips and potatoes, placing dots of butter in between and a sprinkling of salt and pepper. Barely cover with the cream and bake at 350° approximately 1 hour or until the parsnips and potatoes are tender.

Serves 4 to 6.

Rutabaga and Mashed Potatoes

Rutabaga is a deep yellow root vegetable. Look for one about the size of a small head of cabbage. It takes a long time to cook, so cutting it into small cubes will shorten preparation time.

1½ cups rutabaga, peeled and cut into 1-inch cubes
1½ cups russet potatoes, peeled or not, in 1-inch cubes
1 tablespoon butter
2 cloves garlic, minced
3 scallions, whites and a bit of the greens, minced
½ cup half-and-half
salt and white pepper to taste

Boil the rutabaga until it is fork tender, about 15 to 20 minutes. After the first 5 minutes, add the potatoes to the water, and they will be done at the same time as the rutabaga, more or less. In a nonstick skillet, melt the butter and sauté the garlic and scallions for about 2 minutes, until they are soft. Drain the potatoes and rutabaga, place in the bowl of a food processor, and process until they are well pureed. Add the half-and-half, salt, and pepper and pulse a few times until blended with the potato mixture. Taste and correct the seasonings.

Serves 6 to 8.

Broccoli Puree

Maine's northernmost area is Aroostook County, known in the state as "The County." It's here that our famous potato industry flourishes (or, some years, doesn't); 150,000 acres of potatoes are planted each year. The County is as big as Connecticut and Rhode Island combined, and many of its residents have names straight out of the bayous of Louisiana. Their ancestors were all expelled together from present-day Nova Scotia when the British took over in 1755. The ones who settled in The County are Acadians; their Southern cousins are called Cajuns. Broccoli as a cash crop was started a few years back to help even out the vagaries of the potato harvest.

We think even George Bush would enjoy this. It is not for those who are watching their fat intake, but even the diet conscious should be able to fall off the wagon occasionally. A great Thanksgiving side dish.

3 pounds broccoli
1 teaspoon salt (optional)
6 tablespoons melted butter
1 teaspoon freshly ground pepper
1/4 teaspoon nutmeg, freshly grated if possible
3 tablespoons heavy cream
1/4 cup Parmesan cheese, freshly grated if possible

Cut the broccoli in small pieces, separating the florets and the stems. Boil the stems for 10 minutes in the salted (if desired) water, then add the florets and cook until tender.

Drain well and put the broccoli through a food mill or puree in a food processor. Add the butter, pepper, nutmeg, and heavy cream and blend well. Add salt to taste, if desired. Spoon into a 1½-quart baking dish and sprinkle with the cheese. Heat in 375° oven for 10 minutes.

Serves 6.

Easy Broccoli Mold

This is a rich dish and should be served with something simple like grilled fish or chicken.

2 packages frozen chopped broccoli, cooked and drained
1 cup mayonnaise
1 tablespoon butter
1 tablespoon flour
3 eggs
1 cup light cream
1 teaspoon salt

While the broccoli is still hot, mix the mayonnaise and butter with it. Sprinkle the flour over the top. Beat the eggs until light and add to the broccoli mixture. Add the cream and salt and mix all thoroughly. Pour into a greased ring mold or casserole dish. Place the mold in a pan of hot water and bake in a preheated 350° oven for 30 to 40 minutes or until a knife inserted in the center comes out clean. Unmold if in a ring.

Serves 6.

Creamed Spinach

One of the few times we use a frozen vegetable. This is party fare and wonderfully quick and easy. Not low-fat, but worth splurging on.

3 packages frozen chopped spinach
1 cup herbed Boursin cheese (or other creamy, soft cheese)
    at room temperature
2 to 3 tablespoons half-and-half
1 tablespoon grated onion
dash nutmeg
salt and pepper to taste

Defrost the spinach and squeeze out all the moisture. Mix the cheese with enough of the half-and-half so that it can be stirred. In a 3-quart saucepan, mix the spinach, onion, cheese mixture, nutmeg, salt, and pepper. Heat slowly on low heat until hot. May also be placed in a 350° oven and heated for 25 minutes or until hot.

Serves 6.

Corn Oysters

The Down East version of corn fritters.

3 cups fresh corn (off the cob) or frozen kernels
2 tablespoons flour
2 tablespoons butter
2 egg yolks, beaten
salt and pepper to taste
2 egg whites, stiffly beaten
milk, if needed
1 cup vegetable oil (more or less) for deep frying

Make a stiff batter with the corn, flour, butter, egg yolks, and seasonings. Fold in the egg whites last. If the batter seems too stiff to handle, mix in a *very* little milk. Heat the oil to 375° and drop the batter into it by tablespoonfuls and fry until golden brown. Drain the Corn Oysters on paper towels and serve them hot and crisp.

Serves 4 to 6.

Candied Whole Carrots

Another quick and simple recipe that will remind you of days gone by. If you double the amount of carrots, increase the syrup only by half.

1 pound whole baby carrots, scrubbed
4 tablespoons butter or margarine
$\frac{1}{4}$ to $\frac{1}{2}$ cup brown sugar
2 tablespoons undiluted frozen orange juice

Boil the carrots until they are just tender. In a 12-inch skillet, melt the butter or margarine and add the brown sugar and orange juice. Heat for 1 or 2 minutes, stirring until it begins to thicken slightly. Drain the carrots well and add them to the brown sugar mixture. Continue cooking for 3 to 4 minutes or until the syrup has thickened a bit and covers the carrots well. Serve hot.

Serves 4.

Green Tomato Pie

Because summer is short and often ends without notice, green tomatoes are a part of everyone's life in September, especially those of us with home gardens. Here is a great way to use them.

pastry for 2-crust pie
2 cups of green tomatoes, cut in 1/2-inch cubes
pinch of salt
1 tablespoon flour
1 cup sugar
1 tablespoon lemon juice
1 tablespoon butter or margarine
1 teaspoon ground cinnamon
1/4 teaspoon ground nutmeg

Line a 9-inch pie plate with 1/2 of the pastry. Combine the remaining ingredients and fill the pie shell. Roll out the remaining pastry and top the pie. Crimp the edges together and cut 4 1-inch slits in the center. Bake in 350° oven for 45 minutes.

Serves 6.

Corn Flan or Crustless Corn Quiche

A good, hearty dish for lunch or for Sunday supper with a salad and French bread. As long as you're making one, make two and freeze one, either before or after baking.

3 eggs
1 cup whole milk or half-and-half
4 tablespoons melted butter
2 cups frozen corn
½ teaspoon salt
¼ teaspoon pepper
pinch cayenne pepper
¼ teaspoon nutmeg
½ pound Cheddar cheese, thinly sliced
2 tablespoons grated Parmesan cheese

Beat together the eggs, milk, and butter. Stir in the corn and seasonings. Place ½ of the mixture in an 8- or 9-inch pie plate that has been sprayed with vegetable oil. Place a layer of cheese slices on top and spread the remaining corn mixture on top of the Cheddar cheese slices. Sprinkle the Parmesan over all and bake in a preheated 325° oven for approximately 45 minutes or until set. Let stand a few minutes before cutting.

Serves 6.

Tomato Corn Pudding

This is so good that if it's one of those things your mom gave you as a kid, you go through life trying to remember the recipe. We suppose you could use canned tomatoes in this casserole, but the fresh ones make it so much better. In winter use the fresh Italian-style tomatoes. For some reason, they taste more like the real thing than the hothouse varieties.

1 small green pepper, seeded and diced
1 small onion, finely chopped
2 tablespoons canola oil
2 tablespoons flour
pinch salt
pinch cayenne pepper
1/2 cup evaporated milk
1/4 cup grated sharp Cheddar cheese
2 eggs
2 1/4 cups frozen corn
2 firm but ripe medium tomatoes

In a nonstick skillet, sauté the peppers and onions in the oil until they are soft. Blend in the flour, salt, cayenne pepper, milk, and cheese, stirring with a wire whisk until it thickens. Cool for a few minutes. Beat the eggs slightly. Add the cheese sauce and the corn. Pour the mixture into a 1- or 1 1/2-quart casserole. Cook in a preheated 350° oven until nearly firm.

Cut the tomatoes into fairly thin slices and arrange over the top of the corn. Bake the casserole about 10 minutes longer or until the tomatoes are done.

Serves 4.

Grilled Fresh Tomato Slices

*Don't even think about these unless it's tomato season. And when it **is** fresh tomato season, we bet you'll think about them several times a week. Quick, easy, and really wonderful!*

3 large, firm, ripe tomatoes
1 tablespoon minced fresh basil
½ cup (approximately) herbed bread crumbs
2 tablespoons melted butter

Line a cookie sheet with aluminum foil and spray the foil with vegetable spray. Cut the tomatoes into slices between ¾ and 1 inch thick. Arrange them on the foil. Mix the minced fresh basil with the bread crumbs and sprinkle approximately 1 tablespoon on top of each slice. Drizzle a bit of melted butter on each.

Preheat the broiler and place the slices about 8 to 12 inches from the heat. Broilers vary, especially gas ones. You want the tomatoes to cook slightly, but you do not want the topping to burn before the cooking is accomplished. When the bread crumbs are nicely toasted, serve immediately or keep warm in a low oven.

Serves 4 to 6.

Sautéed Carrots and Apricots

Talk about elegant! This is fragrant and has an intense sweetness you'll love. It's the color of the trees in peak season in the fall and is a great complement to game.

5 tablespoons unsalted butter
1 medium onion, very thinly sliced
2 pounds carrots, shredded or julienne cut
4 ounces dried apricots, scissored into thin strips
½ chicken or vegetable stock or water
2 teaspoons sherry vinegar (or raspberry vinegar)
salt and pepper to taste (optional)

Melt the butter in a 12-inch skillet. Sauté the onions until they are golden brown. Add the carrots and apricots and sauté for 2 minutes. Add the stock, cover, and simmer about 5 minutes or until carrots are just tender. Cook, uncovered, until liquid is evaporated. Add the vinegar and the salt and pepper if desired.

Serves 4.

Maine Saturday Night Baked Beans

If you live here, you already know about Maine's baked beans. If you're a visitor, don't miss 'em!

2 cups (1 pound) dried beans (kidney, yellow-eyed, pea, navy, or soldier beans)
½ pound salt pork (fat and lean)
3 teaspoons salt
3 tablespoons brown sugar
2 teaspoons dry mustard
⅓ cup dark blackstrap molasses
2 cups boiling water

Wash and pick over the beans. Soak the beans overnight in water to cover plus 2 inches. Drain. Put the beans into a large pot, add water to cover, and boil until the beans are tender. When some of the skins start to burst, they are ready. Place the cooked beans in a bean pot or other large, heavy casserole with a tight-fitting cover. Alternate layers of beans and pork, sprinkling each layer with a mixture of the salt, brown sugar, and mustard. Over each layer, add a portion of the blackstrap molasses. Pour at least 2 cups of boiling water over all. Bake in a 275° oven for at least 6 hours, replacing the water as it is absorbed. About ½ hour before serving, remove the cover and let the top brown.

Serves 6.

Jamaican Baked Beans

The sound of steel drums can't disguise the Down East origins of this fragrant dish. Rum simply adds a grace note.

1 pound navy beans
1 medium onion, studded with 5 or 6 cloves
½ pound salt pork, cut into 1½-inch pieces
½ cup dark brown sugar
¼ cup dark rum
1 tablespoon dry mustard
1 teaspoon ground lemon pepper
pinch thyme
2 cups chicken or vegetable stock, hot
2 to 3 cups water, hot

Soak the beans overnight in enough water to cover. Drain the beans and add enough water to reach 2 inches above the beans. Simmer 30 to 40 minutes until barely tender.

Place the onion in the center of a large bean pot or earthenware casserole with a cover. Cover the onion with ½ the beans and layer on ½ the pork. Add the remaining beans and then the remaining pork.

Combine the brown sugar, rum, and seasonings; add them to the beans; then add 2 cups of the hot stock and enough of the hot water to barely cover. Put the lid on the pot and bake at 250° for 4 to 5 hours until tender, adding a little hot water if they become dry. Uncover for the last half hour.

Serves 6.

Pig Tails and Beans

Maine grows some mighty fine beans—kidney, lima, soldier,
pigeon, navy, cow peas, black-eyed peas—you name it, we grow
it. For years the only way to cook beans Maine-style was long
and sweet, seasoned with pork and molasses. When Terry
arrived in Hancock with years of Louisiana cooking under her
belt, she devised lots of ways to take advantage of both cultures.
The following is a product of that experience.

1 pound dried butter or lima beans
boiling water
1½ pounds pig tails, cut in small pieces (if no pig tails,
    substitute ham hocks)
1 onion, sliced
1 green pepper, seeded and sliced
1 clove garlic, minced
2 small dried red pepper pods
2 teaspoons salt
1 teaspoon brown sugar
½ teaspoon dried mustard
dash of Worcestershire sauce

Wash and pick over the beans. Place in a large pot and
cover with boiling water. Cook for 2 minutes. Remove from
the heat and let soak for 1 hour or more. Place the pig tails
or ham hocks in another pot and cover with boiling water.
Boil for 30 minutes. Add the onion, green pepper, garlic,
pepper pods, seasonings, and drained beans. Simmer until
tender, adding more hot water during cooking if necessary.

Serves 6.

New Year Cabbage

There's a saying hereabouts that to make doubly sure there will be more money in the new year, a little cabbage helps a lot. Why take chances when you can eat something as good as this?

1 small cabbage
oil
2 tablespoons butter
2 tablespoons flour
1½ cups milk
½ cup grated cheese (Parmesan or your choice)
salt and pepper to taste
celery salt to taste
1 tablespoon chopped parsley
bread crumbs

Cut the cabbage in quarters and boil in salted water until tender. Drain and place in an oiled baking dish. Melt the butter, stir in the flour, and gradually add the milk, stirring with a whisk until thickened. Add ½ of the grated cheese and all of the seasoning to taste. Pour over the cabbage, sprinkle with the chopped parsley and bread crumbs and remaining cheese, and bake in a preheated 350° oven until brown, about ½ hour.

Serves 4.

Zucchini Casserole

Even though the growing season appears to last only ten minutes in Maine, we still seem to end up with more zucchini than we can persuade our friends and neighbors to accept. Here's a solution hearty enough to be a main dish.

3 8- to 9-inch zucchini, sliced
3 tablespoons flour
2 tablespoons olive oil
1 cup rice, uncooked
1 medium onion, finely chopped
$\frac{1}{2}$ cup mushrooms, wiped and sliced
2 cups chicken stock
1 large onion, thinly sliced
1 clove garlic, finely minced
2 large, firm tomatoes, sliced
$1\frac{1}{2}$ tablespoons fresh basil, finely minced
1 cup grated Cheddar cheese

Sprinkle the sliced zucchini with the flour and sauté in 1 tablespoon of the olive oil until lightly browned. Set aside. Cook the rice, medium onion, and mushrooms in the chicken stock in a covered pot until the rice is tender, 18 to 20 minutes. Set aside. Sauté the large onion and the garlic in the rest of the oil until soft, add the tomatoes and fresh basil, and continue cooking 1 or 2 minutes. Be careful not to cook the tomatoes too long or they will turn to mush.

Butter a shallow $2\frac{1}{2}$- or 3-quart casserole and layer first the zucchini, then the rice, and finally the tomatoes. Make two layers of each if you need to. Top with the cheese and bake in a 350° oven for 20 to 30 minutes.

Serves 6.

Minted Peas

2 cups shelled fresh peas (or 2 cups frozen peas)
1 teaspoon fresh mint, minced
½ teaspoon sugar
2 tablespoons butter
¼ cup water (if using fresh peas)
3 or 4 large lettuce leaves

Preheat oven to 350°. In a 1½- or 2-quart casserole, place
all the ingredients except the lettuce leaves and mix gently.
Do not use the water if you are using frozen peas. Wash
the lettuce leaves and layer them over the top of the peas,
covering the entire top surface. Place the casserole in
the oven and bake for 20 minutes for frozen peas or
30 minutes for fresh ones. Remove the lettuce leaves before
serving.

Serves 4.

❋ ❋ ❋

*It takes a while for folks "from away" to realize that
Fourth of July food is not hot dogs or barbecued chicken.
In Maine, Fourth of July means poached salmon with egg
sauce and early peas. The salmon begins to "run" about
this time, and peas are rarely ready for picking till then.*

Quick-and-Easy Tomato Spinach

This is one of those last resort recipes. Ingredients are nearly always at hand and the taste of this combination is so amazing, addiction could follow.

1 medium onion, minced
1 large clove garlic, minced
1 tablespoon canola oil
2 packages frozen chopped spinach, not defrosted
1 8-ounce can tomato sauce
salt and freshly grated pepper to taste

In a nonstick frying pan, sauté the onion and garlic for 1 or 2 minutes in oil until they are soft. Add the frozen spinach and continue to cook until it has separated and most of the water has evaporated. Add the tomato sauce, salt, and pepper and serve.

Serves 4 to 6.

Cauliflower au Gratin

Make sure the other items on your dinner menu are colorful—perhaps a tomato-sauce-topped meatloaf and baked sweet potato—because the presentation of this vegetable is 100% pale vanilla. The taste, however, is deep, rich, and incredible.

1 head cauliflower, rinsed and cut into florets
2 tablespoons butter
2 tablespoons flour
1 cup milk, heated
1 tablespoon dry vermouth
pinch cayenne pepper
1 cup grated sharp Cheddar cheese
pinch salt (optional)
$\frac{1}{2}$ to $\frac{3}{4}$ cup bread crumbs
1 tablespoon melted butter

Steam the cauliflower until tender, about 5 minutes. Drain. In a 3-quart saucepan, melt the butter and add the flour to it, mixing with a wire whisk. Add the warm milk, mixing to keep it from becoming lumpy. Add the vermouth, pepper, grated cheese, and salt, if desired. Stir constantly until the cheese is melted and the sauce is well thickened and creamy. Place the cauliflower in a 2-quart casserole that you have sprayed with a vegetable spray. Sprinkle the bread crumbs over the top and drizzle the melted butter over the crumbs. Bake in a preheated 350° oven for 25 minutes.

Serves 6.

Breads and Muffins

They say that if you are trying to sell your house, you should always have bread in the oven when people come by to inspect the premises. There are few things as fair as the warm, yeasty aroma of freshly baking bread, that's for sure. Bread baking is a big subject, and the recipes we have chosen are those that can be accomplished by a novice baker as well as an experienced one. The most important thing about baking is to enjoy the process as much as the result. Ready, set, go!

Blueberry Muffins

Naturally we use our famous wild Maine blueberries. You can fit a lot more berries into each muffin; and the taste is so intense, it makes those other big, fat berries seem like cardboard.

⅔ cup shortening
1 cup sugar
3 eggs
3 cups flour
3 heaping teaspoons baking powder
½ teaspoon salt
1 cup milk
1 full cup blueberries

Cream the shortening and sugar until fluffy. Add the eggs, one at a time, beating well after each addition. Sift together the flour, baking powder, and salt. Add the dry ingredients alternately with the milk. When blended, add the blueberries. Bake in greased muffin tins in a preheated 375° oven for 15 to 20 minutes.

Makes 12 medium-size muffins.

Sweet Potato Muffins

These sweet, golden treats are as good with a cold roast chicken breast at lunch as they are with fresh roasted coffee at breakfast. Serve them warm.

½ cup butter
½ cup sugar
½ cup packed brown sugar
2 eggs
1¼ cups mashed cooked sweet potatoes
1½ cups flour
2 teaspoons baking powder
¼ teaspoon salt
1 teaspoon cinnamon
¼ teaspoon nutmeg
1 cup milk

Cream the butter and sugars, add the eggs, and mix well. Blend in the potatoes. Sift the dry ingredients together and add alternately with the milk. Be careful not to overmix, as the muffins will be tough. Fill greased muffin tins ⅔ full. Bake in a preheated 400° oven for 25 minutes.

Makes about 12 muffins.

Apple Muffins

One of the loveliest sights along the highways and byways of Maine is the apple trees. We feel sure that Johnny Appleseed must have spent some "quality time" Down East. Feathers of pink and white in the spring, gaunt, gnarled branches loaded with fruit in the fall, sparkling with the icy crystals of winter— Maine's apple trees are a sight to behold. These apple muffins are quintessentially Maine.

1 ½ cups flour, sifted
½ cup sugar
½ teaspoon salt
1 ¾ teaspoons baking powder
½ teaspoon nutmeg
1 egg, beaten
¼ cup milk
⅓ cup salad oil
½ cup grated apple, firmly packed
¼ cup butter or margarine, melted
½ cup sugar
1 tablespoon cinnamon

Sift the first five ingredients together. Combine the egg, milk, and oil and add to the flour mixture. Mix until *just* moistened. Add the grated apple. Fill greased and floured muffin pans ⅔ full. Bake in a preheated 400° oven for 20 to 25 minutes. Brush the muffin tops with the melted butter and roll them in the cinnamon-sugar mixture. Serve warm.

Makes about 9 medium-size muffins.

Carrot and Cornmeal Muffins

Try to forget how "good for you" these must be and concentrate on how fabulous they taste.

1 cup carrots, coarsely grated
1 cup whole wheat flour
1 cup cornmeal
⅓ cup bran
1 teaspoon baking powder
½ teaspoon baking soda
1 cup carrot, orange, or cranberry juice
2 tablespoons butter
1 tablespoon honey
2 eggs, beaten
about 1 cup buttermilk

Combine the carrots and all the dry ingredients. Mix the juice, butter, honey, and eggs. Add as much buttermilk as is required for a smooth batter, mixing gently. Butter large muffin tins. Pour ⅔ full of batter. Bake in a preheated 400° oven for about 25 minutes. These are particularly crunchy if you use large shreds of carrot rather than finely grating them.

Makes about 12 muffins.

Corn Blueberry Skillet Bread

A perfect marriage of Southern charm with Down East character.

1 tablespoon butter
1½ cups white cornmeal
½ cup flour
1 teaspoon baking soda
2 tablespoons sugar
½ teaspoon salt
2 eggs, beaten
1 cup buttermilk
2 cups milk
1 cup Maine wild blueberries, gently rinsed

Melt the butter in the bottom of a 10-inch cast-iron skillet. Sift together the cornmeal, flour, soda, sugar, and salt. Mix in the eggs, the buttermilk, and 1 cup of the milk. Fold in the blueberries and pour into the heated skillet. Pour the last of the milk over the top, but do not stir. Bake in a preheated 350° oven for 50 minutes or until done.

Serves 6 to 8.

Banana Bran Bread

Another "good-for-you" loaf; but now that you know it, you never have to mention it again. This is a perfectly balanced and succulent bread that's a complete breakfast.

1 cup your favorite bran cereal
3 tablespoons canola oil
3 ripe bananas, mashed
½ cup light brown sugar
¼ cup boiling water
1 egg
1½ cups sifted flour
½ teaspoon baking soda
2 teaspoons baking powder

Measure the cereal, oil, bananas, and sugar into a bowl. Add the water and mix well. Add the egg and beat well. Sift the flour, baking soda, and baking powder together; then add to the banana mixture, stirring only until combined.

Spray two 9-by-5-by-3-inch bread pans with vegetable spray and divide the batter between them. Bake in a preheated 350° oven for approximately 45 minutes or until a toothpick tester comes out clean.

Makes 2 loaves.

Dilly Dinner Rolls

This is basically a white dinner roll to which dill adds a fragrant touch. Lovely with chicken, fish, or veal.

1 scant tablespoon dry yeast
¾ cup warm water (100°–110°)
2 tablespoons sugar
1 teaspoon salt
½ cup warm milk
1 egg
¼ cup yogurt
1½ tablespoons fresh dill weed, snipped fine
3½ to 4 cups white all-purpose flour

Place the yeast in a small bowl, add the warm water, and let proof for 5 to 10 minutes. Meanwhile, in a large bowl combine the sugar, salt, and warm milk. Blend the egg, the yogurt, and the dill, and add to the milk mixture, then add all to the yeast mixture. Gradually add the flour, mixing well after each addition so that the batter is well blended. Cover the dough lightly with a towel and let it rise in a warm place until doubled in bulk, about 25 to 35 minutes.

Stir the batter down and spoon into well-greased muffin tins, filling each one about ½ full. Cover loosely and let rise in a warm place until the dough fills the tins, about 35 to 45 minutes. Bake in a preheated 400° oven for 15 to 20 minutes or until done. Remove from the tins and serve warm.

Makes about 18 rolls.

Onion Bread

Sally uses a heavy-duty mixer to make bread; Terry and Bob Rohe use elbow grease. This bread may be made either way, and either way it's a class act.

2 teaspoons dry yeast
1 teaspoon sugar
2¼ cups warm water (about 110°)
⅓ cup instant nonfat dry milk
2 tablespoons corn oil
4 cups all-purpose flour
2 cups whole wheat flour
2 ounces onion soup mix
cornmeal

Place the yeast, sugar, and 2 cups of the warm water in a large bowl. Mix the last ¼ cup of the warm water with the dry milk, add the oil, and add this mixture to the bowl. Mix both flours with the onion soup mix and add to the bowl.

   Knead by hand or with a dough hook for 5 minutes or until the dough loses its stickiness and becomes elastic. Turn into greased bowl, cover with plastic wrap, and place in a draft-free, warm place. Let rise until it is double in bulk.

   Punch the dough down. Divide into 2 loaves or into rolls or baguettes. Sprinkle a baking sheet with the cornmeal. Place the formed dough on the baking sheet and let rise a second time (about 30 minutes). Bake in the center of a preheated 425° oven—15 to 20 minutes for rolls, about 25 minutes for loaves or baguettes.

Makes 2 loaves or about 15 to 20 medium rolls.

Sally Cohen's Breakfast Loaf

This bread makes the best toast in the world—with the possible exception of Bob Rohe's loaves, which follow this recipe.

2 packages (or 2 scant tablespoons) dry yeast
1 cup lukewarm water (105°–115°)
¼ cup honey
¼ cup molasses
1 tablespoon canola oil
2 cups lukewarm milk (made from instant dry skim milk)
1 tablespoon salt
3 cups whole wheat flour
4 cups white flour
¼ cup wheat berries
1 cup oatmeal

In a 2-cup glass measuring cup, mix the yeast and the luke-warm water. Let stand 5 minutes to proof. Add the honey, molasses, and oil to the yeast and water. Pour the mixture into the bowl of a large heavy-duty mixer fitted with a dough hook. Prepare the lukewarm milk in the 2-cup measure and add to the yeast mixture. Add the salt to the whole wheat flour and mix. Pour both flours, the wheat berries, and oatmeal into the mixer bowl and begin mixing. When all flour is incorporated, knead on the machine for about 5 minutes until the dough pulls away from the sides of the bowl and begins to form around the dough hook. You may add more white flour as needed if the dough remains sticky.

Remove the dough from the bowl, place on a floured surface, and knead 1 or 2 minutes by hand. Add small amounts of flour to your board if the dough remains sticky. It is ready when it has become elastic and when it returns to its previous shape if you poke it hard with your finger.

Place the kneaded dough ball in a large, oiled bowl, turning the ball over once to oil the dough as well. Cover loosely with plastic wrap, set in a warm place, and let rise until it is double in bulk.

Punch the dough down and divide it in half. Form each half into a loaf shape and place each in an oiled 9-by-5-inch loaf pan. Cover each loosely and let rise again until the dough has risen above the sides of the pans. Bake in the middle of a preheated 375° oven for 25 to 30 minutes. The bread is done when it has a hollow sound when tapped on the bottom of the loaf. Remove the loaves from the pans and let cool on a wire rack.

Makes 2 loaves.

Robert K. Rohe's Famous Multi-Grain Bread

Terry's husband, Bob, is the principal contrabass player with the Bangor Symphony Orchestra and also a composer of note. However, notes are not all he composes. We think this bread is a masterpiece! Its formula was arrived at after much experimentation.

3 tablespoons dry yeast
3 cups water, body temperature
¾ stick butter (use ¼ stick for greasing the pans)
¾ cup honey
3 heaping teaspoons sea salt
6 eggs
handful sesame seeds
handful millet (Bob has big hands)
½ cup wheat bran
¼ cup soy flour
¼ cup wheat germ
½ cup oatmeal
3 to 4 pounds unbleached, unbromated flour

In a large bowl, add the yeast to the tepid water. Let proof 5 to 10 minutes. Melt the butter, honey, and sea salt in a saucepan over low heat. Beat the eggs, add to the honey mixture, and pour all into the bowl and mix. Add the sesame, millet, bran, soy flour, wheat germ, and oatmeal, and mix.

Start adding the flour, 1 cup at a time, until the dough no longer sticks to the sides of the bowl. Turn out onto a bread board and knead until you have a good, solid, elastic

dough. Wash and dry the bowl and oil it with corn oil.
Place the dough in the bowl and turn the dough upside
down to coat it all over. Cover with a damp cloth and allow
it to rise 1 to 1½ hours or until double in size.

Grease 4 9-by-5-inch bread tins with butter. Flatten
the dough, cut into 4 equal parts, mold each into a loaf
shape, and set into the bread pans. Cover again and allow
to rise until the dough is slightly rounded above the sides
of the pans. Place in a preheated 300° oven and bake 45 to
55 minutes or until nicely brown. Remove from the pans
and cool on a wire rack.

Makes 4 loaves.

Cheese Popovers

Popovers are those huge, warm, crispy-on-the-outside, tender-and-chewy-on-the-inside muffins that look very difficult to make but aren't. Now that we've cleared that up, you have no excuse not to give it a go. You can buy wonderful nonstick popover tins, but oven-proof glass custard cups work just as well. The only prerequisite is that whichever cup you choose should be deeper than it is wide. Fill them only ⅓ full. The batter will quickly rise and "pop over" the sides of the cup, forming a small explosion of a muffin that will melt in your mouth. For plain popovers, simply leave out the cheese.

2 extra-large eggs
1 cup milk
1 tablespoon canola oil
1 cup flour
pinch salt
6 teaspoons grated cheese

Preheat oven to 450°. If the muffin cups are glass or pottery, place them on a cookie sheet and heat them in the oven while you mix the batter. Put into a medium-size bowl the eggs, milk, oil, flour, and salt. Beat with an electric hand mixer until the batter is very smooth. (You can mix it in a blender if you like.) Pour 2 to 3 tablespoons of the batter into the bottom of each cup. Add 1 teaspoon of cheese, then a bit more batter, until the cups are ⅓ full. Bake at 450° for 15 minutes, then turn down to 350° for another 15 minutes. Serve while hot.

Makes about 6 popovers.

Desserts

Have you ever seen the bumper sticker that reads "Life is short. Eat dessert first"? As far as we're concerned, truer words were never spoken. Somehow there seems to be something untrustworthy about a person who claims not to have a sweet tooth. Our dessert collection is an assembly of recipes featuring many of the fabulous things Maine is famous for. Blueberries, cranberries, and apples (in all their many guises) abound, as well as traditional desserts such as Indian Pudding and Pumpkin Pie. And don't think for a moment that we are immune to chocolate on the rocky Maine coast. In fact, if you live in a state where, if spring comes on a Sunday you go on a picnic, chocolate becomes a staple, a necessity of life. We hope you enjoy these treats as much as we enjoyed testing them for you!

Chocolate Amaretto Pie

In putting this recipe first, we're cutting to the chase, as they say on the movie set. We didn't want to put the richest, sweetest, heaviest, darkest, most-elegant chocolate pie somewhere in the middle where you'd have a hard time finding it if you were in a hurry. This is certain to make your reputation. It is the creation of Sally's dear friend, Gayle Winston, who serves it in her wonderful River House Inn in Grassy Creek, North Carolina.

Crust

1½ cups Famous Chocolate Wafer crumbs
2 ounces almond paste
½ stick melted butter

Mix these ingredients in a food processor. Line a buttered 9-inch pie plate with the mixture and bake in a preheated 350° oven for 5 minutes. Cool.

Filling

2 eggs, separated
2 tablespoons strong coffee
2 ounces almond paste
1 tablespoon heavy cream
1 tablespoon brandy
2 tablespoons amaretto
2 tablespoons dark rum
¾ pound (12 ounces) semisweet chocolate
4 tablespoons (½ stick) butter
1 cup minus 1 tablespoon heavy cream
2 tablespoons powdered sugar

In a large bowl, beat the egg yolks until light. Add the coffee, almond paste, 1 tablespoon heavy cream, brandy, amaretto, and rum. Melt the chocolate and butter over warm water. Cool slightly and add to the egg mixture. Beat the egg whites until they are foamy, add the powdered sugar, and beat until they hold soft peaks, then fold into the chocolate mixture.

Fill the crust. There will be ½ cup or more filling left over. Place the leftover filling in a pastry bag fitted with a decorative tip. Pipe the filling around the edges of the pie. Chill for at least 4 hours. Serve with the remainder of the cream, whipped. Freezes well.

Serves 8.

❋ ❋ ❋

Maine pies are simple, but every town, every village has its best pie maker. She's always on call for the covered dish suppers at church or the women's clubs. Don Marquis in his Sonnets to a Red Haired Lady *wrote "I love you, as New Englanders love pie."*

Maine Shaker Cider Pie

Here's a wonderful pie we love to bake in the autumn when fresh cider is abundant. It's a lovely custardy dessert that can be served cold or at room temperature.

2 cups fresh apple cider
1 tablespoon butter
1 cup brown sugar
¼ cup water
¼ teaspoon salt
2 egg yolks, beaten
2 egg whites, stiffly beaten
1 unbaked 9-inch pie shell
1 teaspoon nutmeg

Place the cider in a saucepan and boil gently until it is reduced to ½ cup. Add the butter, sugar, water, and salt. Simmer 5 or 6 minutes. Cool slightly and add the beaten egg yolks. Fold in the stiffly beaten egg whites. Pour into the unbaked pie shell. Dust with the nutmeg and bake in a preheated 350° oven for 20 to 30 minutes or until the crust is brown and custard is set.

Serves 6 to 8.

Mrs. Anna Rogers' Pumpkin Pie

*This is **the** traditional pumpkin pie. No Nouvelle Cuisine here, just good eating.*

1 ¼ cups cooked pumpkin, fresh or canned
½ teaspoon ground ginger
½ teaspoon cinnamon
¾ cup sugar
1 ¾ cups milk
1 heaping tablespoon flour
1 egg
pinch salt (optional)
1 single pie shell, partially baked

Cook all the ingredients in the top of a double boiler until thick. Pour into the partially baked pie shell and bake in a preheated 350° oven for 20 minutes.

Serves 6 to 8.

Surprise Pumpkin Pie

This really is a lovely pie. The nuts in the crust give it an unexpected texture, and the spicy streusel adds another interesting dimension to an old favorite.

pastry dough for 1 9-inch pie crust (homemade or
    prepared)
1¼ cups finely chopped pecans
1 egg
1 30-ounce can pumpkin or 3½ cups fresh, cooked
    pumpkin
1 can sweetened condensed milk

If making the pie crust from scratch, add the pecans to your dough ingredients. If using a prepared shell, press the chopped nuts into the shell after you have placed it in the pie tin. Blend the egg, pumpkin, and condensed milk and pour the mixture into the pie shell. Sprinkle the streusel on the pie and bake in a preheated 375° oven for 50 to 55 minutes or until a knife inserted in the center comes out clean.

Serves 8.

Streusel Topping

¼ cup packed brown sugar
¼ cup flour
½ cup chopped pecans
¼ cup firm butter

Mix all the ingredients with a fork or pastry blender until crumbly.

Aunt Lucy's Raspberry Pie

This is one of the prettiest pies you'll ever see. If you can, get some fresh raspberries to sprinkle on top.

1 12-ounce package frozen raspberries
1 package raspberry gelatin
3 eggs, separated
1 tablespoon lemon juice
pinch salt
¼ cup sugar
1 cup heavy cream, whipped
1 graham cracker or chocolate wafer crust in a 9-inch pie
    plate, baked for 5 minutes

Thaw and drain the berries, reserving the juice in a measuring cup. Add water to make ¾ cup. Bring the juice to boiling and pour over the gelatin, stirring until the gelatin is dissolved. Remove this mixture from the heat. Beat the egg yolks until they are light and add them to the gelatin mixture. Add the berries, lemon juice, and salt and mix gently. Chill until half firm.

Beat the egg whites, adding the sugar slowly, until they hold soft peaks. Fold the beaten whites into the half-firm gelatin, then fold in the whipped cream. Mound in the pie shell, sprinkle with fresh raspberries if available, then refrigerate until ready to serve.

Serves 8.

Cousin Charlotte Windsor's Raisin and Cranberry Pie

Cousin Charlotte was a pleasant maiden lady from Brookline, Massachusetts. She created this wonderful old-fashioned pie recipe which is probably close to a century old. It has a deep, pungent aroma and flavor, and is a perfect addition to a holiday meal.

1 heaping tablespoon cornstarch
1 cup water ($\frac{3}{4}$ of it boiling, $\frac{1}{4}$ cold)
2 cups cranberries, chopped
1 cup raisins, chopped
1$\frac{1}{3}$ cups sugar
pinch nutmeg
2 prepared or homemade pie crusts
1 tablespoon butter

Dissolve the cornstarch in the $\frac{1}{4}$ cup cold water, then slowly add the boiling water, stirring constantly. Mix together the cranberries, raisins, sugar, and nutmeg. Add the thickened hot water. Place 1 crust in the bottom of an 8- or 9-inch pie plate. Add the fruit mixture, dot with the butter, and place the other crust on top, crimping the edges. Make about a dozen 1-inch slashes in a pattern on the top crust. Bake in a preheated 425° oven for 20 minutes, then turn the oven down to 350° and bake for another $\frac{1}{2}$ hour until the filling is bubbly and the crust is golden brown.

Serves 6 to 8.

Spiced Blueberry Pie with Curaçao

2 9-inch pie crusts
5 cups Maine wild blueberries
¾ cup sugar
4 tablespoons flour
¼ teaspoon allspice
1 teaspoon cinnamon
3 tablespoons curaçao liqueur
2 tablespoons butter or margarine

Place 1 crust in the bottom of a 9-inch pie plate. In a large
bowl, mix together the blueberries, sugar, flour, allspice,
cinnamon, and curaçao. Pour the berry mixture into the pie
shell and dot with the butter. Place the second crust over
the pie, seal the edges, and prick a design in the top crust
with a sharp knife so that the steam can escape. Bake in a
preheated 450° oven for 20 minutes until the pie begins to
brown. Turn the oven down to 350° and bake for 35 to
45 minutes more, until the filling is bubbly. Serve warm or
at room temperature, either plain or with vanilla ice cream.

Serves 8.

Winter Fruit Compote Jim

You won't believe the aroma that will fill your kitchen while this is baking. Don't be put off by its dark, lumpy appearance. Just add a dollop of vanilla ice cream and savor the flavors. Our friend Carol Skinner dreamed this one up.

½ cup dried, pitted apricots
½ cup dried, pitted prunes
2 tart, unpeeled apples, cored and diced
1 large pear, cored and diced
2 plums, pitted and diced
1 banana, peeled and diced
¼ cup dates, chopped
¼ cup white raisins
½ cup walnuts, coarsely chopped
6 tablespoons dark brown sugar
1 teaspoon cinnamon
2 tablespoons butter or margarine
grated zest of 1 lemon
juice of 1 lime
¼ cup Jim Beam, Wild Turkey, or other good bourbon

Place the apricots and prunes in a saucepan, add water to cover, and simmer for 5 minutes. Let the fruit cool in the liquid. Mix the apples, pear, plums, and banana. Dice the cooled apricots and prunes, reserving the liquid. Mix the dates, raisins, and nuts with the sugar and cinnamon, then mix it with the rest of the fruit.

Put ½ of the fruit in a 3-quart casserole. Dot with
1 tablespoon of the butter or margarine and sprinkle on ½
the lemon zest and ½ the lime juice. Add the remaining
fruit, dot with the rest of the butter or margarine, and
sprinkle on the last of the lemon zest and lime juice. Mix
the reserved cooking liquid and the bourbon and pour it
over the fruit. Bake in a preheated 325° oven for approximately 1 hour or until the fruit is very soft. Stir once during
the baking. Serve lukewarm with whipped cream or ice
cream.

Serves 6.

Maine Wild Blueberry Crisp

Maine's absolutely unique wild blueberries are becoming famous all over the world. The bushes grow low to the ground and turn an unbelievable russet color in the autumn. Half the size of cultivated berries and with an intense flavor, ours are harvested with short-handled rakes by entire families who work together in late July to bring in the one harvest per year of this precious crop. Visitors can arrange to pick their own. It's hard on the back, but worth it!

3 cups fresh Maine wild blueberries
1 tablespoon fresh lemon juice
1½ cups your favorite granola
4 tablespoons whole wheat flour
½ cup brown sugar
1 teaspoon cinnamon (if granola doesn't contain any)
¼ cup canola oil

Gently rinse the berries, sprinkle with lemon juice, and pour into a 1½-quart baking dish sprayed with vegetable oil. In a mixing bowl, combine the granola, flour, brown sugar, cinnamon, and oil. Mix well and spread over the berries. Bake in a preheated 350° oven for about 40 minutes until the berries are bubbling and the topping is brown. Serve with vanilla ice cream or yogurt.

Serves 5 or 6.

Maple Apple Dumplings

Why don't people make dumplings any more? They're easy, they're fun, and they taste great.

2 cups sifted flour
1½ teaspoons baking powder
1 teaspoon sugar
½ teaspoon salt
½ cup apples, peeled, cored, and chopped
¾ cup milk
2 cups maple syrup
1 tablespoon water

Mix all the dry ingredients together with a wire whisk. Add the cored, chopped apples and the milk to the dry ingredients and mix well. Bring the maple syrup and the water to a boil. Drop the apple batter by tablespoonfuls into the boiling maple syrup. (Kindly suggestion: wear padded mitts; hot maple syrup can spatter, and when it does, it smarts!) Cook the dumplings for 10 minutes in the syrup, which must be boiling all the time. Serve in small dessert dishes, letting the dumplings swim around in a little pool of syrup.

Makes about 24 plump dumplings; serves 6.

Old-Fashioned Apple Crisp

When life gets to be too much and you need to get in touch with the inner you, try this.

2 teaspoons cinnamon
2 teaspoons nutmeg
1 teaspoon allspice
1 cup brown sugar
5 or 6 tart, firm medium-large apples, cored, peeled, and
    sliced
6 tablespoons butter
½ cup whole wheat flour
½ cup oatmeal
¼ cup cider (or water, but cider is better)

Butter a deep 2-quart baking dish. Mix the cinnamon, nutmeg, allspice, and brown sugar together. Place the apples in the baking dish and sprinkle ½ of the cinnamon mixture on top of them. Dot with two tablespoons of the butter.

Add the flour, oatmeal, and the remaining butter to the rest of the cinnamon mixture and stir with a fork until well combined and crumbly. Spread this mixture over the apples. Add the cider or water and dot with the remaining butter. Bake in a preheated 350° oven until the apples are soft and the crust has gently browned, about 30 to 35 minutes. Serve warm with plenty of sweetened whipped cream or French vanilla ice cream.

Serves 6.

Oatmeal Cookie Pie Crust

Sheila Daley lives with her husband, Chipper, and their two Newfoundlands in a house that Chip designed and built for them in Gouldsboro, Maine. Sheila is a grand cook and has a file full of healthful and delicious recipes she shares. This is Sheila's recipe, and it can be used interchangeably with any kind of cookie crumb pie crust. It's wonderful with creamed pies, chocolate pies, fruit pies, and chiffon pies and is delicious filled simply with fresh, uncooked fruit.

1 1/2 cups raw rolled oats
1/4 cup sesame seeds
1/2 cup whole wheat flour
1/4 teaspoon salt (optional)
1/2 teaspoon cinnamon
1/4 cup finely minced nuts
1/2 teaspoon vanilla extract
3 ounces butter or margarine, melted, or substitute
    canola oil
3 tablespoons honey, mixed with the butter or oil

Combine all the ingredients (may be done in a food processor) and press firmly and evenly into the bottom and sides of a 9- or 10-inch pie plate. May be prebaked at 350° for 8 minutes if you are going to use a precooked or uncooked filling. In this case, cool before filling. Otherwise, fill with the desired filling and bake according to recipe instructions.

Makes 1 9- or 10-inch pie.

Carla's Lemon Cake

Carla Anderson, a long-time friend of Sally's mother, parted with this unusual recipe. When we first read this recipe, we said, "It'll never fly." But you better believe it does. It serves a dozen or more people; is tart, sweet, and delicious; and has the most amazing texture.

1 package lemon gelatin
1 cup boiling water
4 eggs
¾ cup vegetable oil
dash salt
1 box Betty Crocker Lemon Velvet cake mix
butter and flour for pan

Dissolve the gelatin in the cup of boiling water and stir until the graininess is gone. Cool. Break the eggs into a large bowl and beat them lightly. Add the vegetable oil and salt to the eggs. Add the cooled gelatin to the eggs and mix well. Add the cake mix to the gelatin and mix thoroughly.

Butter and flour a 9-by-13-by-2½-inch rectangular baking pan. Pour the batter into the pan and bake in a pre-heated 350° oven for 30 to 45 minutes or until a toothpick tester comes out clean. Remove from the oven and place the pan on a wire rack. Pierce the top of the cake all over with a toothpick and pour the Glaze over the top. This cake tastes best if made and glazed a day or two before you are going to serve it.

Serves about 15.

Glaze

2 cups powdered sugar
½ cup lemon juice
grated zest of 1 lemon

Mix the ingredients and pour over the Lemon Cake. Cover and serve a day or two later, if possible.

Aunt Sally's Chocolate Ice Box Cake

You can use any good semisweet chocolate for this tender dessert. The original version, we believe, was on the Baker's German Sweet Chocolate bar wrapper in the 1940s. Kids adore it, so make an extra one if there are children with access to your refrigerator.

8 ounces semisweet or German Sweet chocolate
3 tablespoons water, coffee, or orange liqueur
2 eggs, separated
1 cup heavy cream
1 tablespoon powdered sugar
18 double ladyfingers or a small angel food cake
1 cup heavy cream, sweetened with a tablespoon of
    powdered sugar, for frosting (optional)

Melt the chocolate in the top of a double boiler. Add the water and coffee or liqueur and blend well. Add the egg yolks to the sugar and mix thoroughly, then cool. Beat the egg whites. Whip the cream and powdered sugar. Fold the whites and then the whipped cream into the chocolate mixture.

Line a loaf pan with waxed paper. Place a layer of ladyfingers or thinly sliced cake over the paper, lining both the bottom and sides of the pan. Fill the remainder of the space inside the cake with the chocolate mixture. Put a final layer of cake or ladyfingers on the top of the chocolate. Refrigerate for at least 2 hours.

Near serving time, unmold the cake, peel off the waxed paper, and frost, if desired, with the additional whipped cream.

Serves 8.

World's Best Brownies

Sally's daughter, Maggie, came up with the frosting innovation. This is another of our top-ten "most requested" recipes—you can't eat just one.

2 eggs
1 cup sugar
½ stick butter
2 squares bitter chocolate
½ cup flour, sifted
1 teaspoon vanilla
½ cup chopped walnuts or pecans
1 box thin chocolate-covered mint candies

In a medium bowl, mix the eggs and sugar. Melt the butter and chocolate together in a saucepan or double boiler over simmering water. Add, alternately, the flour and the butter mixture to the egg mixture. Add the vanilla and nuts. Bake in a preheated 350° oven for 28 (for fudgey) or 30 minutes.

While the brownies are still hot, cover the top with a layer of the chocolate candies. They will quickly melt, at which point spread the goo over the top of the brownies.

Makes 12.

222 Good Old-Fashioned Maine Cookery

Aunt Gert's Chocolate Cake

Aunt Gert was Sally's grandmother's aunt. Her chocolate cake recipe was in a handwritten recipe book given to Sally's mother by her mother-in-law upon her marriage. This recipe is over 100 years old. It's simplicity itself, and thus one you can feel free to call upon when you feel the need to make something life-affirming.

1½ cups brown sugar
½ cup softened butter
1 egg
4 tablespoons cocoa
2 cups flour
1 teaspoon baking soda
1 cup buttermilk
1 teaspoon vanilla

Cream the brown sugar and the butter. Add the egg and mix well. Mix the cocoa, flour, and baking soda together with a whisk. Add the buttermilk and flour mixture alternately to the butter mixture. Add the vanilla and mix.

Butter and flour 2 8-inch layer pans. You may fit a cut circle of parchment or waxed paper into the bottom of each pan to make removal easier. Pour the batter into the prepared pans and bake in a preheated 350° oven for ½ hour or until a toothpick tester comes out clean. Frost with Chocolate Wonder Frosting.

Serves 8 to 10.

Chocolate Wonder Frosting

1 8-ounce package of cream cheese, at room temperature
2 to 3 tablespoons milk
2 squares unsweetened chocolate
pinch salt
2 cups powdered sugar
1 teaspoon vanilla

Place the cream cheese and milk in a medium-size bowl.
Melt the chocolate in the top of a double boiler over
simmering water. Using a hand mixer, combine the milk
and cheese until they are blended. Add the chocolate and
continue mixing until it is completely incorporated. Add
the salt and the powdered sugar, a few spoonfuls at a time,
until the desired consistency is achieved. Add the vanilla
and mix well. If the frosting is too thin, add more powdered
sugar; if too thick, add milk.

Frosts an 8- or 9-inch layer cake.

Applesauce Cake

If you're watching the amounts and kinds of fat in your diet, try substituting ¼ cup canola oil for the butter in this recipe. Butter will give it a special flavor, but the applesauce will keep it nice and moist, so either way this cake is a winner.

1 teaspoon baking soda
1 tablespoon warm water
1 cup tart applesauce
½ cup sugar
½ cup molasses
½ cup butter
2 cups sifted flour
¼ teaspoon salt (optional)
½ teaspoon powdered cloves
½ teaspoon cinnamon
¼ teaspoon allspice
1 cup seeded chopped raisins

Dissolve the soda in the warm water and stir into the applesauce. Combine all the other ingredients and stir them into the applesauce. Beat thoroughly and turn into a buttered 9-inch tube pan. Bake in a preheated 350° oven for 30 minutes or until a cake tester comes out clean.

Makes 1 cake.

Maple Mousse

Yes, chocolate mousse is sublime, raspberry mousse is an inspired way to end a midsummer dinner—but just wait until you taste Maple Mousse!

3 eggs
¼ cup water
1 envelope unflavored gelatin
¾ cup maple syrup
¼ cup granulated sugar
1 cup heavy cream
1 tablespoon confectioner's sugar

Separate the eggs and set the whites aside. Place ¼ cup of water in the top of a double boiler and sprinkle with the gelatin; let stand until softened. Add the maple syrup and the egg yolks, stir to blend, then cook over simmering water, stirring constantly until the gelatin dissolves and the mixture begins to thicken. Remove from the heat, transfer to a cool bowl, and refrigerate until the mixture is moderately thick.

Beat the egg whites with the ¼ cup of granulated sugar, adding the sugar very gradually. Beat until the whites hold peaks. Beat the heavy cream with the confectioner's sugar, then fold the beaten whites and beaten cream into the custard. Pour into a serving bowl or individual glasses and refrigerate until ready to serve.

Serves 6 to 8.

Cider Sherbet

Even though sherbet is usually thought of as a warm-weather dessert, you should make this in October when fresh apple cider is abundant. Cider sherbet is a grand way to top off a roast pork tenderloin or roast herbed chicken dinner. The flavor of just-picked apples will amaze your guests and have them begging for seconds.

4 cups fresh apple cider
½ cup sugar
1 cup fresh-squeezed orange juice
juice of 1 lemon
2 egg whites

Simmer the cider and sugar together for 5 minutes. Cool. Add the juices and place in the container of an electric or hand-turned ice cream freezer. Follow the manufacturer's instructions until the juices have reached the consistency of mush. Add 2 stiffly beaten egg whites, return to the freezing container, and continue processing until firm. Store in the freezer and remove about 10 minutes before serving. Stir briefly for a smooth consistency.

Serves 6 to 8.

Fresh Peach Ice Cream

There are two ways to do this: the ice cream machine way or the freezer tray way. There is little difference in the final product, so do whichever you find easier. The window of opportunity for peaches in Maine is about three weeks in August. The ice cream is at its peak for only about a week after you make it. It is incredibly good and will spoil the store-bought variety for you forever. This basic recipe will work for many other fruits.

6 to 10 ripe peaches, enough to make 2 cups of pulp
1¾ cups sugar, more or less, to taste
2 cups whipping cream

Peel, pit, and slice the peaches. Process them for about 5 seconds in a food processor. Add the sugar to taste and pulse until just mixed. Whip the cream. Fold the fruit and sugar into the cream. Remove the dividers from 2 metal ice trays or use any shallow freezer-proof pan. Pour the fruit into the pans and then place in the freezer.

When the ice cream has begun to freeze around the edges of the pan but is still soupy in the center, remove it from the freezer and beat with a hand mixer until it is well mixed. Spoon into plastic containers with tight-fitting lids (you will have about 1⅓ quarts) and freeze until ready to use. Remove from the freezer about 10 minutes before serving.

Serves 6.

Fresh Fruit Compote with Caramel Cream Sauce

It's not a true (cooked) caramel, but Caramel Cream Sauce is one of those mysterious concoctions that drive people crazy trying to figure out how it's made! It's one of our most requested sauces. Plan to prepare this the day before you want to serve it. It will keep for up to a week in the refrigerator.

Fresh Fruit Compote

6 to 8 cups of assorted fresh seasonal fruit, peeled or not, cut in bite-size bits
1/4 cup orange liqueur

Our favorite fruits are apples, pears, cherries (pit them, please), strawberries, peaches, melons, and raspberries. Sometimes we do a mix of colors; sometimes we go monochromatic, using honeydew, pears, green grapes, and green apples (unpeeled), or oranges, cantaloupes, peaches, and pineapple. Put the cut-up fruit in a beautiful glass serving bowl and sprinkle the top with the orange liqueur. Refrigerate until ready to serve with the sauce.

Serves 8 to 10.

Caramel Cream Sauce

1 cup heavy cream, whipped
1 cup sour cream
½ to ¾ cup dark brown sugar, packed

After whipping the cream, mix in the sour cream, then add the brown sugar to taste. Refrigerate at least 4 hours—overnight, if possible. Stir before serving. This is also great over gingerbread, plum pudding, chocolate soufflé; or use your imagination!

Serves 8 to 10.

Orange Bread Pudding

There are dozens of versions of bread pudding, most all of them good. It's a great way to use up old bread, and when you use a raisin loaf or a cinnamon bread, it's especially delectable. Here's a basic recipe to get you started.

3 cups scalded milk
3 tablespoons orange brandy
1 teaspoon grated orange zest
8 to 10 slices of stale bread, buttered on 1 side, then cut
    into ½-inch cubes
4 tablespoons butter
⅓ cup dark brown sugar
3 extra-large eggs, lightly beaten
¼ cup white seedless raisins (optional)
1 teaspoon cinnamon
1 teaspoon nutmeg

Remove the scalded milk from the heat and add the orange brandy and orange zest. Set aside. Put the buttered bread cubes into a buttered 6- or 8-cup casserole. Add the brown sugar, eggs, raisins, cinnamon, and nutmeg to the cooled milk and pour it over the bread. Let the bread soak for 30 minutes. Dot well with the butter.

Set the casserole in a pan of hot water about 1 inch deep and bake it in a preheated 375° oven for 50 minutes to an hour or until set. Serve with whipped cream, heavy cream, or vanilla ice cream.

Serves 6.

Gingersnaps

Who doesn't remember these? Gingersnaps must still be loved, or the commercial cookie companies wouldn't keep making them. These will make the store-bought variety pale in comparison. Great keepers, too.

1½ cups heavy cream
2½ cups firmly packed brown sugar
¾ cup molasses
½ cup dark brown corn syrup
1 tablespoon ground ginger
grated zest of 1½ lemons
2 tablespoons baking soda
8 to 9 cups flour
decorative sugar icing, if you wish

Whip the cream until almost stiff. Combine the sugar, molasses, corn syrup, ginger, lemon zest, and baking soda and mix thoroughly. Pour this mixture into the whipped cream and beat 10 minutes by hand or 4 minutes with an electric mixer. Add 5 cups of the flour and blend. Slowly blend in the remaining flour until the dough is just smooth enough to handle but still pliable. Wrap in waxed paper and chill, preferably overnight.

Remove from the refrigerator and roll out the dough on a floured board to ¼-inch thickness. Cut into your favorite shapes with cookie cutters. Place on a lightly buttered cookie sheet and bake in a preheated 375° oven for about 12 minutes or until golden brown.

If you believe in gilding the lily, make a glaze of 1½ cups confectioner's sugar and enough orange juice to make the sugar spreadable, and lightly frost each cookie.

Makes about 5 dozen cookies.

Nanny's Chocolate Cookies

Sally got this recipe from her grandmother. It made her a chocoholic at age seven.

1 cup brown sugar
1 well-beaten egg
1 stick melted butter
½ teaspoon baking soda
1 tablespoon boiling water
2 cups flour
4 tablespoons cocoa
½ cup milk
1 cup chopped pecans

Mix the sugar and egg together in a large bowl. Add the melted butter and stir well. Dissolve the baking soda in the boiling water and add to the sugar and egg mixture. Sift the flour and cocoa together and add them to the sugar and egg mixture alternately with the milk. Add the nuts. Drop by teaspoonfuls on a greased cookie sheet. Bake in a preheated 350° oven for 10 to 12 minutes or until done. The cookies will be puffy. Frost while still warm.

Makes about 36 cookies.

Frosting

4 tablespoons cocoa
1 cup powdered sugar
1 heaping tablespoon soft butter
2 to 3 tablespoons (more or less) brewed coffee

Sift the cocoa and sugar together in a small bowl, then add the butter and mix until well blended. Add the coffee 1 spoonful at a time, until the right consistency has been reached.

Frosts 36 cookies.

Double Crunch Bars

A great favorite of the kids in the family. Also wonderful for picnics or to take out on the boat.

4 cups quick oatmeal, uncooked
1½ chopped walnuts
1 cup brown sugar, firmly packed
¾ cup melted butter
½ cup honey
1 teaspoon vanilla
1 teaspoon salt

Combine all the ingredients and mix well. Press firmly into a 10½-by-15½-inch jelly roll pan. Bake in a preheated 450° oven for 10 to 15 minutes or until golden brown and bubbly. Cool thoroughly and cut into 1-inch-by-2-inch bars.

Makes approximately 24 bars.

Date Bars

These are so chewy and sweet, they will soon be a family favorite. Packed into metal tins, they make great Christmas gifts—if you have any left.

2 cups brown sugar
2 tablespoons butter
2 eggs
2 tablespoons water or orange juice
2 teaspoons vanilla
1 cup flour
1 teaspoon baking powder
$\frac{1}{2}$ teaspoon cinnamon
$\frac{1}{4}$ teaspoon ground cloves
2 cups chopped dates
$\frac{1}{2}$ cup chopped pecans or walnuts
powdered sugar

Grease an 8-inch-square pan, line the bottom with wax paper, and grease the paper too. Combine the sugar and the butter. Add the eggs and beat thoroughly. Add the juice or water and the vanilla. Combine and toss together the flour, baking powder, cinnamon, and cloves and add them to the butter mixture. Mix until combined. Stir in the dates and nuts. Pour into the prepared pan and bake for about 25 minutes until firm and lightly browned. Cool 5 minutes. Turn onto a rack and peel off the wax paper. Cut while warm into 1-inch-by-2-inch bars. Roll in the powdered sugar and store in a dry place or freeze. They will keep for days and days.

Makes about 20 bars.

Chocolate Pears

We started the chapter with chocolate, and we can't think of a better way to end it than by more of the same. This wonderful dish has the added merit of giving you something to do with your sweet cider when it has gone 'round the bend.

4 firm pears with stems
1½ cups hard cider
2 tablespoons sugar
1 cup semisweet chocolate bits

Leaving the stems intact, thinly peel the pears. Core them carefully from the bottom, leaving the fruit whole. Put the cider and sugar in a saucepan and heat slowly to a simmer. Add the fruit and poach gently for about 15 to 20 minutes. Remove from the heat before the fruit becomes too soft. Drain and dry on a paper towel, reserving the syrup.

Melt the chocolate in a bowl over hot water. Coat the fruit with the chocolate, either by dipping them or by spooning the chocolate over the pears. Serve in individual dishes or on a serving platter. Top with the reserved syrup or with ice cream.

Serves 4.

Index

International Conversion Chart

These are not *exact* equivalents; they've been slightly rounded to make measuring easier.

Cup Measurements

American	Imperial	Metric	Australian
¼ cup (2 oz)	2 fl oz	60 ml	2 tablespoons
⅓ cup (3 oz)	3 fl oz	84 ml	¼ cup
½ cup (4 oz)	4 fl oz	125 ml	⅓ cup
⅔ cup (5 oz)	5 fl oz	170 ml	½ cup
¾ cup (6 oz)	6 fl oz	185 ml	⅔ cup
1 cup (8 oz)	8 fl oz	250 ml	¾ cup

Spoon Measurements

American	Metric
¼ teaspoon	1 ml
½ teaspoon	2 ml
1 teaspoon	5 ml
1 tablespoon	15 ml

Oven Temperatures

Farenheit	Centigrade
250	120
300	150
325	160
350	180
375	190
400	200
450	230